WHAT LEADERS ARE SAYING ABOUT *10*...

I've known Dennis for over 25 years and watched him lead one of the more unique churches in America with over 140 different nationalities. This book, *10*, defines the key that unlocks the power of the church to impact the world by moving people from believers to disciples!

— **John Maxwell, The John Maxwell Co.**

The Bible talks a lot about being a disciple of Jesus, but how does that apply to us today? In this book, Dennis Rouse breaks it down into simple terms and explains what it *really* means to be a disciple. I have been friends with Dennis and his wife, Colleen, for many years, and I know what he has to say about discipleship will transform your life. If you're a believer looking to take your relationship with the Lord to a new level, this is the book for you!

— **Robert Morris, Founding Senior Pastor of Gateway Church, Bestselling Author of *The Blessed Life, Truly Free*, and *Frequency***

If I had this book in my formative years as a Christian believer, I would no doubt be a better disciple today. In *10*, Dennis Rouse "the Pastor" comes from behind the podium, steps down from the platform, sits on stool and teaches us 10 authentic traits of a mature Christian disciple. Like me, you'll be gripped by the compelling authenticity and biblically based pragmatic steps leading us to be a 10. Individuals and small groups will grow to a 10, and so will God's Kingdom.

— **Sam Chand, Leadership Consultant and author of *Bigger, Faster Leadership***

Dennis Rouse is one of the leading pastors in America and has built a dynamic church full of passionate disciples. This book spells out the practical steps of how average believers can become world-changing followers of Jesus. This passion is what's missing in much of the church today. I believe every Christian should read this book, and all pastors should use these principles to teach their members to be true disciples of Jesus.

— **Jimmy Evans, Author of *Marriage on the Rock* and *The Right One*, Founder of Marriage Today**

10: Qualities that Move You from a Believer to a Disciple takes us on the journey to engage in the vibrant life of the fully committed. This transformation is not rooted in our performance, but in our realization of the love of God. Dennis's passion is contagious. You will love the practical guidelines that serve as tools to help us take steps forward. Thank you, Pastor Dennis, for marking this path for all of us to follow!

— **Lisa Bevere, *New York Times* Bestselling Author of *Without Rival***

One of the greatest challenges of being a Christian is keeping our relationship with Jesus as our life's primary passion and purpose. In *10*, Dennis Rouse challenges us to take an honest look at our faith and shift from simply believing in Christ to actively walking with Him each and every day. Drawing from his own faith experience and thoughtful insights from God's Word, Dennis shares practical ways we can all grow closer to Jesus and truly live as His disciples and not just as believers.

— **Chris Hodges, Senior Pastor, Church of the Highlands, Author of *Fresh Air* and *The Daniel Dilemma***

10 will help you take your church family to a whole new level of discipleship. What Dennis has shared will fuel the passion, love and commitment of true disciples so we can be the salt and light for the Lord in our world.

— **Tom Mullins, Founding Pastor, Christ Fellowship, Palm Beach Gardens, Florida**

I'm not a person given to political rhetoric or exaggerated words of acclaim. With that simple fact established, I will tell you that Dennis Rouse's book *10* should be "required reading" for the 21st century church. It genuinely exudes passion, vulnerability, courage, and authenticity. Even more importantly, each chapter emanates from a focused sense of biblical accuracy and refreshing practicality. Individual believers and small groups will be inspired with renewed purpose to be a biblical "10"—both in their personal character development and in their pursuit of Christ. In a church culture that has sadly allowed talent to become an acceptable substitute for genuine anointing, *10* stands in a league of its own. Postpone reading this book at your own peril.

— **Jeanne Mayo, Founder & President of Youth Leader's Coach and The Cadre, Author, Speaker, and Director of Youth & Young Adult Outreach at Victory World Church, Norcross, Georgia**

As a rule, a book is rarely more powerful than the author. When I met Dennis, our friendship was immediate and easy. As I watched God build a great church under his leadership, I saw Dennis walk with a depth that was powerful. This book comes from a man who lives the principles it describes. No wonder it is transforming lives! Read the introduction. I'm convinced it will be enough to pull you into the whole journey. This book is personal, biblical, accessible and life-changing. It's the kind of book you read for yourself, then you'll take it into your small group, and then into your circle of friends!

— Kevin Myers, Founding Pastor, 12Stone Church, Lawrenceville, Georgia, Co-author of the best-selling book, *Home Run*

Dennis is an amazing pastor who has created an incredible resource for Christians. His book *10* provides a succinct way to bridge the gap between information and transformation. In our society, we are inundated with increasing volumes of data, and information sharing has become the false positive of genuine growth. In contrast, *10* goes to the heart of the issue: it addresses the key biblical principles of personal change. This book translates discipleship into a practical template which anyone can apply. I wholeheartedly recommend it. *10* is a must-read. Dive in; you won't be the same. Dennis has knocked it out of the park!

— Gerald Brooks, D.D., D.C.L., Founding Pastor of Grace Outreach Church, Plano, Texas, Author of *The Building Blocks of Leadership*

When a man condenses his lifetime of pastoring to 10 life-changing principles, you need to listen. Dennis Rouse has the character, integrity, and pastoral clout to speak about discipleship. His motivation in writing this book is to raise up a new generation of disciples, and not just attenders. Prepare for a powerful, time-tested curriculum of personal spiritual growth . . . that can change our nation.

— Larry Stockstill, Teaching Pastor at Bethany Church, Baton Rouge, Louisiana, Author of *Cell Church, The Remnant* and *Model Man*

One of the greatest needs in today's church is a resource that explains to the believer that a relationship with Christ involves a life of genuine discipleship. For many, the decision to follow Christ is the first and last step, but actually, it's only the first. In this book, Pastor Dennis accurately communicates the life of discipleship for every follower of Christ.

— Joe Champion, Lead Pastor, Celebration Church, Austin, Texas

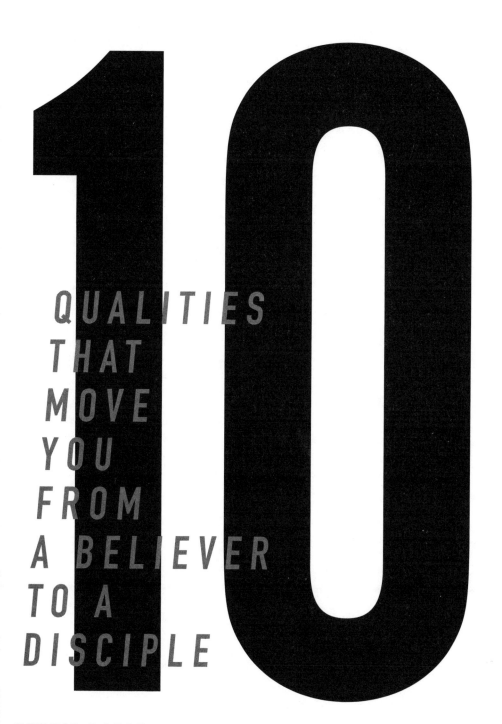

10

QUALITIES THAT MOVE YOU FROM A BELIEVER TO A DISCIPLE

DENNIS ROUSE

FOREWORD BY JOHN BEVERE

Jacket design by Chad Price and the Victory Experience Team.
Interior layout and formatting by Anne McLaughlin.

ISBN: 978-1-947505-01-8
Published by Baxter Press
First printing 2017
Printed in the United States

CONTENTS

FOREWORD

My wife Lisa and I have had the honor of being close friends with Pastor Dennis and his wife Colleen for over twenty-five years. They are both on our Board of Directors. They not only help us with Messenger International's administrative direction, but they also serve as part of a small group of pastors who oversee and speak into our lives.

Lisa and I have had the privilege of meeting and getting to know numerous leaders in our travels. Over the years, we've learned it's not the gift or anointing on a leader's life that matters most; rather, it's the life they lead in private that gives enduring success. We've spent a lot of time with Dennis and Colleen and have observed their constant commitment to live close to Jesus and reflect His character. It's a daily process, and they do it beautifully.

Dennis and Colleen lead a very large and diverse community of believers who are passionate followers of Jesus. They understand there is so much more to being a disciple than just professing to belong to Jesus, showing up to church on Sunday, or periodically reading a few scriptures. We are called into a relationship with God, and through that intimate relationship, we become His disciples.

Too often we depend on a set of rules to give us a predictable outcome. Dennis reminds us that it's not about the rules, but instead, it's about the relationship. God wants us to enjoy the journey with Him. He wants us to experience His love, and He wants to teach us how to be His followers. When Jesus walked with His disciples, He showed them how to live. We have that very same opportunity.

God invites us to enjoy a richer, fuller life with Him, and as a result, to change our world. What greater calling can we ask for? As you read, I encourage you to press in and be expectant. This book will refresh your soul and give you a new perspective on what it means to follow Jesus.

I'm so grateful Pastor Dennis wrote this book. I'm confident that these pages will bring you closer to God in a way that empowers you to be a passionate and devoted follower of Christ!

— John Bevere
   Bestselling Author and Minister
   Cofounder of Messenger International

INTRODUCTION

We're about to take a journey! Not just an ordinary journey, but a journey into the very heart of what it means to move from merely being a *believer* in Jesus to becoming His fully committed *disciple!*

The only reason you would read this book is because you're searching for something more than you've experienced with God. In fact, that was my journey. Many years ago, I started studying the life of Christ and realized that much of what we call Christianity is sadly lacking in substance and passion. In other words, many Christians aren't true reflections of Jesus to the world. This book was born from a burden I've had for many years: I've watched the church slowly slide away from the challenging values and high purposes of Jesus to the misguided conclusion that our purpose is only to feel better about ourselves—even if we're not living out the plan God designed for us.

In John's prophetic book, Revelation, Jesus warned that a church was becoming lukewarm because its people had traded their passion for God for worldly pursuits. I want you to take a moment before you read any further and ask yourself, "Where am I in my relationship with God? Am I just a believer in Jesus who does 'the church thing' every now and then as long as nothing else comes up, or am I passionately pursuing what it means to be a fully committed disciple of Christ?"

Don't answer too quickly. Think about it. And it might help to ask yourself how Jesus would answer this question about you.

TURNING POINT

Years ago, I was at a crisis point in my faith. Something was wrong, but I couldn't put my finger on it. I was trying really hard to please God, but I felt dry, burned out, used up. I drove up to the mountains in North Georgia to be alone, fast and pray, and see if I could figure it out. Sometimes in all our busyness, we can drift away from God's grace as the source of our joy and strength. At the time, everything in my life looked good on the outside. The church I was pastoring was experiencing incredible growth, and people's lives were being touched around me every day in a very powerful way, yet I felt like I was running on empty most of the time. After I arrived at my hotel, I walked out on the balcony and looked out across the beautiful mountains. I began to realize I needed to push the reset button on my life and allow God to talk with me.

As I began to pray, I felt like God asked me a question, "How do you feel about yourself right now?"

I told Him, "I feel empty. I just don't feel like I measure up to what You expect out of me!" After a few moments of silence, I was even more honest. I said, "I'm battling the sense I'm losing my passion for You!"

Then the Lord said, "How do you think I feel about you?"

Instantly I blurted out, "Disappointed."

I sensed the Lord telling me, "What you're experiencing is very common. It's Satan's plan for people to define themselves by their successes and failures instead of My unconditional love, forgiveness, and acceptance. When that happens, they eventually feel condemned, pressured, and hopeless. That's the trap: defining your life by how well you measure up to some standard of performance instead of My grace and love. Every struggle you have in your flesh is a result of moving away from My love. When you try to earn approval by performance, shame will crush you and drive you away from Me."

That was it! That's the answer!

The reason we sin after we've been born again is that we've moved away from God's love. Without His love, we're left with only our performance to define us. When we succeed—at least, more than other

> "When you try to earn approval by performance, shame will crush you and drive you away from Me."

people—we feel superior. When we fail, guilt and shame dominate our hearts and cloud every thought, action, and relationship. At that point, everything we do is an attempt to fill the void created by the absence of God's love. Addictive behaviors—food, drugs, alcohol, sex, shopping, obsessive entertainment, and all the rest—are meant to anesthetize the pain. This emptiness, this nagging feeling of not measuring up, makes us desperate. Some of us give up, but sensitive and conscientious people try to make up for their failures by doing penance: feeling bad enough long enough. But they can never do enough to fill the gaping hole and heal the open wound. Only the powerful touch of God's love can do that.

The Lord reminded me of something Jesus told His followers on the night He was betrayed: "As the Father has loved me, so have I loved you. Abide in my love" (John 15:9, ESV). I had gotten it so wrong. I had tried to work really hard to earn God's love so I could feel accepted, but that was exactly backwards. Jesus wanted me to bask in the warmth and strength of His love—the same love the Father has for Him—and never leave that heart-filling, life-changing reality. I can only truly love people and serve God when I live in the revelation of God's amazing love.

MY HOPE FOR YOU

Throughout this book, I'm using two terms that need clear definitions. Many people believe in Jesus, but few are true disciples. A *believer* is someone who gives intellectual assent to the truths of the Bible and may occasionally feel close to God, but *disciples* are so overwhelmed by those truths and the reality of God that everything in their lives revolves around Jesus. If you're reading this book, you're probably at least a believer. My prayer is that by the time you finish reading this book, you'll be on a journey to become a disciple of Christ!

The Christian life is far more than a list of rules God wants us to follow. Yes, He has given us laws and commands, but even more, He has given us himself. Love not only covers a multitude of sins; it also inspires us to want to please the One who has proven His love by giving His life for us. In the same conversation between Jesus and His followers, He explained that the source of power and motivation isn't rule-keeping and guilt. He told them, "These things I have spoken to you, that my joy may be in you, and that your joy may be full" (John 15:11, ESV).

> I told God, "I want to live in Your joy all day, every day."

That day in the mountains, it clicked. I told God, "I want to live in Your joy all day, every day."

And He connected the dots for me: "You'll live in My joy if you abide in My love."

That's the "secret" of being and remaining a disciple who overflows with the love and power of God. That's what I've learned about following Jesus, and that's what this book is all about.

CHAPTER 1

A DISCIPLE IS . . .
PASSIONATELY COMMITTED TO JESUS

In 1981 when I was 22 years old, I left Georgia to start a new business with my father in northern New Jersey. We were designing a unique line of nautical furniture to sell in a niche market that was very popular along the Northeast coastal areas. From the very beginning, our business was successful, and I found myself living the kind of life that I had always envied—traveling to beautiful resort areas, meeting lots of interesting people, and partying my life away! At the time, I was very far away from God, even though my mother had taken me to church all through my teen years. I believed in Jesus, I thought the Bible was a good book, but I didn't want to live that kind of life.

While on a business trip to Richmond, Virginia, to show our furniture, I met a young man named Gene Johnson. He was the perfect example of how to share Christ with someone. He just started up a conversation with me that had no religious overtones at all. In fact, at the end of the day, he came back and started helping me load up my van. When we finished, he invited me out to dinner. As we ate together that night, he began to share his journey with God. It was so disarming that I just sat and took it all in. After dinner he asked me where I was staying. When I told him I was at a nearby hotel, he offered to let me stay at his apartment for the rest of the time I was in Richmond. It was one of the most generous and spontaneous offers I'd ever received, and I decided to take him up on it to save some money.

Over the next couple of weeks, Gene's home became my home. Every night when we both got back—him from his job and me from the show—we talked about life. During those relaxed and friendly conversations, Gene told me about his relationship with Jesus. It wasn't like anything I'd heard before.

After I finished my work in Richmond, I traveled to Atlanta to visit my family and take a few days to have some fun with my friends. I spent the last night with one of my former college roommates. All I can say about that evening was that if there's anything you can do in Atlanta on a Saturday night, we did it! I had a strange feeling that I needed to "go all out" because I might never do this again. (Later, I looked back on that night and realized it was the enemy's last attempt to keep me from surrendering to God.)

The next morning was a Sunday. I woke up in a drunken stupor and announced to my friends that I was going to visit a friend in Stone Mountain who was pastoring a church. My friends just looked at me in disbelief. They didn't understand how we could have done everything we did the night before, and I now wanted to go to church! There was no use explaining it to them, so I just left.

When I got to the church, my pastor friend was really glad to see me. He made sure I sat near the front so I wouldn't miss anything. His church has a tradition of asking someone in the congregation to stand up and end the service with a prayer. To my amazement, he introduced me to the church and asked me to pray. I'm not sure what I said in that moment, but I'm pretty sure at least part of my prayer was: "God, forgive me for last night and bless this church!" It was one of the most awkward moments of my life, but somehow, I made it through and was on the road back to New Jersey that afternoon.

As I began the drive home, I had no idea that my life was about to change drastically in only a few hours! Somewhere on the highway in North Carolina, the atmosphere in my van suddenly changed. All I can explain is that I felt the presence of God all around me. No matter what I tried to do, I couldn't resist the incredible love I was feeling . . . in spite of all I had done the night before. I had heard people talk about "the irresistible grace of God," and that's exactly what I was experiencing. It seemed like no matter how hard I was trying to run from God, He just wasn't going to leave me alone until I surrendered to Him. When I read later in the Bible how the Apostle Paul was converted on the road to Damascus, I could really relate to his experience.

> **As you read this book I want to challenge you to stop disqualifying yourself and let God do with you what He wants to do!**

The next few hours seemed like minutes, and I found myself stopping in Richmond for the night to tell my friend Gene what was happening to me. When we met that night, he immediately launched into a prophetic word, telling me that God had His hand on me and that I would eventually become a pastor of a unique church which would change thousands of lives! I remember looking at him like he'd lost his mind. I told him I would never be a pastor because I was a businessman, and besides, I had done too many bad things in my life to qualify for any kind of ministry for God. Later, I learned that God never calls the qualified, but instead, He qualifies the called. God can take people who seem like nothing and turn them into people who can do something very significant—only because God puts His hand on them. As you read this book I want to challenge you to stop disqualifying yourself and let God do with you what He wants to do!

When I got home, I wasn't sure what to do next. All I knew to do was read my Bible and try to pray every day. For some reason, I had an unusual passion to learn as much as I could about God and find out how to be a better person. Almost on a daily basis, I shared my story with people I met, and to my surprise, many of them accepted Christ. They asked me to help them get closer to God. Seeing God use me was both surprising and exhilarating. I had a strong desire to give something to God, so I started sending money to the church Gene attended, even though I had no understanding of tithing or giving. I usually sent about twenty percent of whatever my business was clearing in profit, and I enjoyed making my business grow so I could increase my giving every month. (I've never understood why so many people struggle to give to their local church. I always thought that if you have a true love for God and even the slightest gratitude for all He's done for you, the least you can do is support His church, but I've realized not everyone thinks like me.)

For almost a year I told people my story, tried to help them grow in their faith, and sent money to Gene's church, yet I still didn't attend a church. Then one morning I heard God say, "I want you to sell your business, move to Richmond, and help a small church." I would discover that the church was a new one where my friend Gene had started attending.

I would also soon learn what Jesus meant when He said that in order to follow Him, you would have to be willing to forsake your family, friends, and even your own life. The passage of Scripture that became a "life word" to me is when Jesus told His disciples, "For whoever desires to save his life will lose it, but whoever loses his life for my sake will find it" (Matthew 16:25). This passage explains why so many Christians struggle with their relationship with God—they're still trying to hold on to their lives even while asking God to give them a new life. I discovered that one of the keys to move from a believer to a disciple was to let go of everything I had trusted in and allow God to rebuild the foundation of my heart!

THE INVITATION AND THE CHALLENGE

When we read the Bible, we soon realize that God longs for a relationship with us, and He will pursue us until we give Him some sort of response. In Paul's letters to the churches, he says we were helpless, hopeless, enemies of God . . . "But God is so rich in mercy, and he loved us so much, that even though we were dead because of our sins, he gave us life when he raised Christ from the dead. (It is only by God's grace that you have been saved!) . . . God saved you by his grace when you believed. And you can't take credit for this; it is a gift from God. Salvation is not a reward for the good things we have done, so none of us can boast about it" (Ephesians 2:4–5, 8–9, NLT).

But that's not all. When we experience the new birth, the new creation, God makes us His "masterpiece" (Ephesians 2:10, NLT). We are drawn to God by His great grace, and then He sends us out with the incredible privilege of representing Him in everything we are, everything we say, and everything we do.

But as we continue to read the Bible, we also realize that following Jesus is the most demanding, difficult assignment of our lives—if we take Him seriously. He doesn't want part of us; He wants all of us. He created us, He paid our debts for us, and He has given us our freedom, but He expects us to use our freedom to honor Him in every possible way.

We often hear people say they like the Sermon on the Mount because Jesus shows us how to live. Yes, He shows us how to live in that famous message, but anyone who really reads it will be shaken to the core! Jesus explains that half measures and flawed motives have no place in a disciple's life. He told His hearers (and us):

"Enter by the narrow gate; for wide is the gate and broad is the way that leads to destruction, and there are many who go in by it. Because narrow is the gate and difficult is the way which leads to life, and there are few who find it. . . . Not everyone who says to Me, 'Lord, Lord,' shall enter the kingdom of heaven, but he who does the will of My Father in heaven. Many will say to Me in that day, 'Lord, Lord, have we not prophesied in Your name, cast out demons in Your name, and done many wonders in Your name?' And then I will declare to them, 'I never knew you; depart from Me, you who practice lawlessness!'" (Matthew 7:13–14, 21–23)

Are you paying attention to what Jesus is saying? He says there are people who are emotional about their faith, who are active in ministry, and who in fact perform miracles, but whose hearts have never been transformed by the gospel of grace. This passage was a warning to those on the hillside in the first century, and it's a warning to us today: Don't mistake occasional emotions, regular church attendance, and effective service for a real relationship with God! Jesus was drawing a powerful distinction between believers and disciples.

This isn't a small matter. Recent research by the Barna Group found that more than nine out of ten people in America believe Jesus was a real person, but only four in ten said they had experienced saving faith in a born-again experience.[1] And even when that more committed group was asked to define and describe their hopes for the future and their goals in life, the vast majority mentioned their careers, their families, and their hobbies—and said nothing about fulfilling God's purpose for their lives. It would appear that very few people who claim to be Christians rank knowing, loving, and following Jesus as their Number 1 priority. Most are believers, but not disciples. Look at the differences:

BELIEVERS . . .	DISCIPLES . . .
1. Believe in Jesus as their Savior but live to please themselves	Believe in Jesus as Lord and live to please God

All of us begin our walk of faith because we need to receive forgiveness and acceptance from God, but many of us never grow beyond the perception that God exists for our benefit. Disciples turn the corner; they realize they've been blessed so they can be a blessing to others. They live to honor the One who has rescued them from death and given them hope for the future. Disciples don't focus only on what God can do for them; they long to give to God and to others.

2. Exalt their opinions, feelings, and thoughts above the Word of God	Exalt the Word of God above their opinions, feelings, and thoughts

Believers focus only on the passages that promise what God will do for them, but disciples take seriously the whole counsel of God. Disciples follow God whether they agree with God's Word or not, whether they understand or not, and whether obeying is easy or not.

3. Think of church as a place they go to *hear* what God's Word say	Think of church as a place they learn to *do* what God's Word says

Many people go to church to be entertained, and they complain when the sermon isn't as interesting as they'd like. Disciples have open ears and eager hearts as they listen. They plan to take action on what they hear from God.

4. **Are accountable only to themselves**   **Are accountable to everyone**

Believers prefer to keep honest feedback at arm's length, but disciples are open to instruction and correction.

5. **Serve God if it's convenient**   **Serve God based on conviction**

Many people give and serve, but only if it doesn't cost them very much. Disciples give, love, and serve like Jesus—even at great cost.

6. **Try to impress God by being religious**   **Seek to know God through a relationship**

Believers and disciples appear to do many of the same activities, but their motives are miles apart. Many Christians try to impress God (and those around them) by being involved in church and service, but disciples do those same things to know God better and reflect His goodness and greatness to everyone.

7. **Follow God as long as everything is going well**   **Follow God regardless of the circumstances**

Believers and disciples have very different breaking points. Believers stick around as long as God seems to be blessing them and life is easy, but disciples keep pursuing God and trusting Him even when their world is falling apart.

| 8. Choose their own path and ask God to bless it | Ask God to reveal the path, and they follow it |

Believers are self-focused. They determine their own goals, and they expect God to help them achieve them. Disciples start with God's will, God's purposes, and God's heart. They look to Him for direction, and they are eager to follow His leading.

| 9. Are full of pride if they're doing well and self-pity if they're not | Are full of gratitude because God's love never fails |

If a person's identity is tied to performance, then pride or self-pity are the rollercoaster they ride all day, every day. But if the grace of God is their source of identity, they find security, strength, and peace even in difficult circumstances.

| 10. Follow the example of the world that seeks to go higher | Follow the example of Jesus to humbly go lower |

The natural mind always wants more power, prestige, and possessions, but the spiritual mind of disciples follows the self-sacrificial example of Jesus.

After His resurrection and before His ascension to the right hand of the Father, Jesus left His followers with a mandate called the Great Commission: "All authority has been given to Me in heaven and on earth. Go therefore and make disciples of all the nations, baptizing them in the name of the Father and of the Son and of the Holy Spirit, teaching them to observe all things that I have commanded you; and lo, I am with you always, even to the end of the age" (Matthew 28:18–20). He gave us a clear directive—not to make believers, create impressive organizations, or build beautiful buildings, but to make disciples in every nation of the world.

How well are you accomplishing this mission? Are you building disciples? Are you one yourself?

DON'T HIRE JESUS TO DO YOUR MARKETING!

I can imagine that many people were perplexed as they saw and listened to Jesus when He traveled from town to town. They marveled as He healed the sick, restored the skin of lepers, gave sight to the blind, and cast out demons. They delighted when He argued with the harsh religious leaders and made them look foolish. And they were thrilled when He turned a boy's sack lunch into a feast for thousands! They saw Jesus as the answer to their greatest hopes. They believed He was going to fulfill all their desires. But then He told them, "If anyone comes to Me and does not hate his father and mother, wife and children, brothers and sisters, yes, and his own life also, he cannot be My disciple. And whoever does not bear his cross and come after Me cannot be My disciple" (Luke 14:26–27).

There's that word again: *disciple.* If Jesus wanted to keep a crowd's attention, He needed some help with His marketing strategy! But maybe He had a different goal than popularity. Maybe He was more interested in building true disciples than being wildly attractive.

In this short statement, Jesus makes two blunt and astounding points. Don't miss them. He says that those who want to be His disciples have to "hate" the people in their families, the people they naturally love most. Don't misunderstand. He's not commanding His followers to be cruel to people. That would be the opposite of everything He has lived and taught! But He's making a stark comparison: Our love, our devotion, and our priority of honoring Jesus should be so strong that our love for family members will look like "hate" in comparison. Yes, we love them, but we love Jesus far, far more. When we put anyone higher than Jesus in our hearts, we may be believers, but we aren't disciples.

The second startling part of Jesus' statement is that His disciples will pick up their crosses and follow Him. Today, we wear crosses on necklaces and as tattoos, but in the first century, the cross wasn't jewelry or art—it was an instrument of state-sponsored torture. Only the worst criminals and traitors were condemned to suffer such a horrific and slow form of execution. When Jesus said that His disciples would be people of the cross, He was explaining the hard truth that following Him comes at the greatest cost and with the most severe sacrifice. Being a disciple isn't for the fainthearted.

> When we put anyone higher than Jesus in our hearts, we may be believers, but we aren't disciples.

The paradox is that salvation is a free, wonderful gift from God's hand, but receiving it costs us everything. God doesn't want just an hour on Sunday morning. He doesn't want just a few minutes of prayer and a verse or two in the morning. He doesn't want a few dollars and a few hours here and there to prove you're a good Christian. He wants everything you've got. Your body is His. Your career is His. Your money is His. Your family is His. Your time is His. Your talents are His. It all belongs to Him because *you* belong to Him.

Does this sound harsh? Does Jesus seem too demanding? A lot of people think so. Being passionately committed to Jesus isn't always fun and warm and wonderful. Often, we see Him do amazing things in people's lives, and we sense His power and love flowing through us. But there are other times when staying true to Jesus demands the deepest sacrifice at the greatest cost. That's when we find out if we're really committed to Him or if we were only along for the ride.

PASSION PRODUCES . . .

Passion is a word we hear in many different contexts. It can describe sex, the desire to excel at work, or an intense commitment to any pursuit. It's a strong or extravagant feeling about a person or a goal, an emotion that motivates us beyond normal existence. Some people may insist, "I'm not passionate about anything." I doubt it. Almost all of us have at least one thing that captures our hearts and is the goal that everything in our lives revolves around. Some of us are passionate about our families, getting to the next position in our careers, or cheering for our favorite teams. Others are consumed with the thirst for revenge or for escape from the pain and emptiness of their lives. Our passion is the pursuit that dominates our hearts and choices. Our highest goal and our biggest dream always push their way to the front of our minds.

Before I trusted Christ, I was a passionate sinner. I lived to drink and party, and I tried to make plenty of money to be sure I could do anything I wanted to do. I was also passionate about the Georgia Bulldogs. At football games in the fall, I dressed in red and black, shouted from the beginning to the end of the game, and lived and died with each play. If the Dawgs won, I drank with my friends to celebrate. If they lost, we drank to numb the pain.

When I became a Christian, God put himself in the center of my heart, and I became a passionate disciple of Jesus Christ. I realized some of those things—money, girls, crazy friends, booze, and Georgia football—needed to become secondary instead of primary. Others were distractions that needed to go.

I also realized there weren't many people in the church who were passionate about Jesus. Every week, I stood next to people who, if they sang at all, only mumbled the words of praise to our great God. And during the sermon, they looked like they were thinking about anything but God's amazing truth. My guess is that when they walked out the door each Sunday, they didn't think about God until the next Sunday morning.

So, what is it that turns a bored and self-absorbed believer into a passionate disciple of Christ? We could identify many different turning points, but I've found three to be the most significant.

1. Pleasing God takes precedence over pleasing people.

We've looked at the passage where Jesus said that our love for Him must be so strong that love for our families will look like hate in comparison. In many families, parents and other relatives are thrilled when someone turns to Jesus, and they're even thrilled when that person takes steps toward being a true disciple . . . but not always. When I became a Christian and told my father I wanted to sell my part of the company to him so I could move to Richmond, my grandmother blew a gasket! She asked me, "Dennis, have you lost your mind? You're a Rouse, so act like a Rouse. We don't act like Jesus freaks. We go to church, but that's it. The Bible is a book of fairy tales! You have a life to live. Don't waste it on Jesus!"

I tried to explain to her that the Bible makes it very clear that Jesus is to be our first priority, and I intended to follow Him no matter where He leads. She sneered, "If you go in that direction, I never want to see you again!" She told me to leave her house immediately, and I did.

I'm not the only one who has had to make hard decisions to please God when others objected. Many single people have to decide between a romantic relationship and Jesus. Some parents have told their kids they've been brainwashed by the Bible and the people in the church. But putting family before Jesus isn't just a problem for new Christians. Anyone can easily put a husband or wife in front of Christ, living to please the spouse more than living to please God. And even more often, parents can put their children at the center of their hearts, a passion that feels good and right and normal, but one that can create conflict in the marriage and even with the children who must be controlled to make the parents look good.

Moving from being a believer to a disciple changes the pecking order of relationships. When we put Jesus first, a few will applaud, many will be confused, and some will conclude we've lost our minds. Count on it. At some point, though, every believer will have to decide what's more important: pleasing God or pleasing people.

2. We follow God regardless of the cost.

When we trust in Christ, we receive unimaginable blessings from God: forgiveness, new life, purpose, peace, joy, and the promise of being in His presence for all eternity. But following Him always comes at a cost . . . a great cost. Jesus told two stories about people who started projects but failed to calculate the cost. A builder needed to carefully look at his plans and materials to be sure he could finish what he started, and a king had to assess the strength of his army to determine if he could defeat an enemy. After telling these stories, Jesus turned to those who were following Him and said, "In the same way, those of you who do not give up everything you have cannot be my disciples" (Luke 14:33, NIV).

God has a way of putting His finger on the one thing we're most reluctant to give up. For Abraham, it was his son Isaac. God had miraculously given Abraham and Sarah a son even though they were far past the age of having children. Isaac was a miraculous gift from God, but gradually, the gift threatened to become more important to Abraham than the giver. God told Abraham to take Isaac up on a mountain and sacrifice him. We can imagine the excruciating journey as the old dad led his son to the top of the mountain, tied him to the wooden altar, and raised the knife above him. Suddenly, God stopped him: "Do not lay your hand on the lad, or do anything to him; for now I know that you fear God, since you have not withheld your son, your only son, from Me" (Genesis 22:12). It was the supreme test of Abraham's life, and he passed it.

The Bible describes many different tests of devotion to God. The rich young ruler was sure Jesus would praise him for his obedience to the law, but Jesus pointed out that money still had a hold on the young man's heart. Peter had been the chief spokesman for Jesus, but when his own life was threatened, he denied that he even knew Him. All of us have that "one thing" we don't want to give up—the person, behavior, or possession we hope God won't ask for. He may not ask for it right away, but He always gets around to it. A disciple gives up everything so that nothing gets in the way of all the love, power, and effectiveness God can provide.

Money was that "one thing" for me. When God told me to sell my part of the business and move to Richmond, He was putting His finger on what I treasured most. Money gave me freedom, pleasure, and security. I was making a lot of money, and God was telling me to give it all up so nothing hindered my devotion to Him. It was the hardest thing I've ever done, but it wasn't the only time God had to deal with me in this way.

After Colleen and I got married, we were living in Richmond, and we had nothing beyond the bare necessities. I looked for a job that would pay more than I was making, and I landed an interview with a company for a position that would pay a significant salary and commissions. The interview was to last about three hours. In the middle of it, we took a break. Suddenly, the Lord said to me, "What are you doing? Why are you in this interview?"

I answered, "Because I'm married and I need to provide for Colleen." After a second or two, I expanded my reasons: "God, this is an incredible opportunity! I can make more money than I've ever made before. It will enable Colleen and me to have the kind of life I've always dreamed of!"

I thought that was indisputable logic, but God then told me plainly, "This isn't what I've called you to do. I have bigger things for you than this." I took a deep breath, and then God said, "It's time for you to excuse yourself from this interview."

I felt embarrassed, but I did it. I walked back into the interview room and announced, "I'm sorry, but I've changed my mind. I don't think this job is right for me. Please excuse me."

The next day, the pastor of the church called me and said, "Dennis, the Lord told me to hire you as part of our church staff. I don't really know what role you'll play, but I believe He wants you to join us." (I later discovered I would be the church secretary and be responsible for all the things no one else wanted to handle.)

Then he added, "We can only pay you $12,000 a year." At that moment, it began to sink in that if I was going to obey God, I was going to have to adjust my thinking about money. After talking to the pastor, I told Colleen about the conversation. We both agreed this job was what I was supposed to do.

When God puts His finger on the "one thing" we're reluctant to give Him, we can find a million excuses to hold it back. Each time we refuse, our passion for Jesus is encrusted by a new layer of apathy and disobedience. But thankfully, when we respond by giving Him that one thing, everything shifts in our relationship with God. Is it worth surrendering everything to God? It's a question we answer every day.

Is it worth surrendering everything to God? It's a question we answer every day.

Believers assume everything about the Christian life should be fun and easy; disciples know a price must be paid. In perhaps his most famous book, *The Cost of Discipleship*, the courageous German pastor Dietrich

Bonhoeffer gave this piercing commentary on a walk of faith: "When Christ calls a man, he bids him come and die."[2] If we don't understand this truth, we'll always remain believers instead of disciples. This is one of the most important principles in spiritual life: we won't discover what God has planned for us until and unless we surrender our grip on our own plans.

3. Life becomes extraordinary.

One of the most important principles of spiritual life is the upside-down nature of being passionate about Jesus. To be great, serve selflessly. To be filled, empty yourself. To have true riches, give generously. To save your life, give it all to God. People are afraid that being totally devoted to Jesus will make them weird (and to be honest, we all know some pretty strange Christians!), but actually, passionate devotion to Jesus results in more love and power than we ever imagined we could experience. Life isn't dull or bitter anymore; it becomes extraordinary!

After Paul described the gospel to the Christians in Rome, he explained that God's grace radically transforms our motivations, our desires, our thoughts, and our direction. Under the Spirit's control, even our normal, everyday life is filled with the adventure of following the King! Paul wrote:

So here's what I want you to do, God helping you: Take your everyday, ordinary life—your sleeping, eating, going-to-work, and walking-around life—and place it before God as an offering. Embracing what God does for you is the best thing you can do for him. Don't become so well-adjusted to your culture that you fit into it without even thinking. Instead, fix your attention on God. You'll be changed from the inside out. Readily recognize what he wants from you, and quickly respond to it. Unlike the culture around you, always dragging you down to its level of immaturity, God brings the best out of you, develops well-formed maturity in you. (Romans 12:1–2, MSG)

When the passion of Jesus fills our hearts, we aren't ordinary workers any longer; we're extraordinary in our attitudes and determination to perform well. We aren't ordinary bosses any longer; we lead with grace, wisdom and patience. We aren't ordinary spouses, parents, or friends any longer; we give and love and serve, not to win approval, but because the love of God overflows from us. We aren't ordinary neighbors anymore; we step out of our comfort zone to engage the people around us. It all begins when we see ourselves through the extraordinary lenses of God's eyes. Here's how He sees us: "But you are a chosen generation, a royal priesthood, a holy nation, His own special people, that you may proclaim the praises of Him who called you out of darkness into His marvelous light" (1 Peter 2:9).

An extraordinary connection with God produces an extraordinary identity, an extraordinary security, an extraordinary joy, and an extraordinary desire for God to use us.

WORTH IT?

If you've read this far and you still wonder if being passionate about Jesus is worth it, my friend, you might still be just a believer. The blessing of a conscience bathed in the forgiveness of God is magnificent, the blessing of having real relationships instead of manipulating and being manipulated is wonderful, and the blessing of seeing God use you to touch the lives of others is thrilling.

Jesus promised to fill our lives with a hundred times more than anything we've lost from following Him. He wasn't talking about dollars or possessions or investments. He was talking about the value of the kingdom of God over the kingdom of man. When we make Jesus our priority over other people, when we're willing to pay the price to follow Him, and when we let Him make our lives extraordinary, we experience the adventure of a lifetime. Nothing else comes close.

Where does this passion come from? We've already identified the source. We can't manufacture zeal for God, and emotions are fickle. Our passion for Jesus is a response to His passion for us. The writer to the Hebrews explained, "Let us lay aside every weight, and the sin which so easily ensnares us, and let us run with endurance the race that is set before us, looking unto Jesus, the author and finisher of our faith, who for the joy that was set before Him endured the cross, despising the shame, and has sat down at the right hand of the throne of God" (Hebrews 12:1–2).

What was the joy set before Jesus that compelled Him to endure torture and death? Was it the splendor of heaven? No, He had all that before He came to earth. Was it a close relationship with the Father? No, He had that long before the beginning of time. The one thing Jesus didn't have before He came to earth was you . . . and me. He endured the cross because He was passionate about us. We are His treasure. When our hearts are amazed at this fact, we'll be passionate about Him because He'll be our treasure.

The message of God's amazing grace comforts us and frees us, but if we really understand it, this message also challenges us to our core. Jesus paid the price for us, so He now owns us: we were bought at a

Now, we don't belong to ourselves, other people, or any other organization or pursuit. We belong to Him, so a disciple prays, "Jesus, fill me, command me, use me. I'm yours!"

steep price! Now, we don't belong to ourselves, other people, or any other organization or pursuit. We belong to Him, so a disciple prays, "Jesus, fill me, command me, use me. I'm yours!"

So, where are you in this transition? Are you a disciple? Do you want to be one?

At the end of each chapter, you'll find a few questions to stimulate your thinking and provide topics for group discussion. Don't rush through these. The goal isn't to fill in the blanks and move on. Instead, take time to think deeply and listen for the voice of the Spirit.

THINK ABOUT IT:

1. Which of the differences between a believer and a disciple stand out to you? Why are these significant?

2. What are some reasons why being a believer is more attractive and comfortable to a lot of people? Which of these reasons have been (or still are) attractive to you?

3. What are some real choices we have to make when we are committed to please God more than the people around us?

4. What are some examples of the "one thing" people try to hold back from God? What is that one thing in your life? What will you do about it?

5. Who do you know who is an example of a passionate disciple of Christ? What about that person is attractive to you? What about that person scares you?

6. And I'll ask the questions from the end of the chapter: So, where are you in this transition? Are you a disciple? Do you want to be one? Why or why not?

7. Rate yourself on a scale of 0 (none) to 10 (totally) to measure how much you are passionately committed to Jesus. Explain your answer. What needs to change?

CHAPTER 2

A DISCIPLE HAS . . .
EXTRAORDINARY LOVE FOR PEOPLE

One of the things that breaks my heart—and I'm sure breaks God's heart, too—is that so many people are turned off by Christians. I often hear people say, "I like Jesus, but I don't like the people who claim to follow Him." They see us as angry, demanding, and judgmental, and they want to stay as far away as possible. What's the problem? What's creating this deep divide between God's people and the rest of society?

I believe this is the reason: We don't know how to love the way Jesus loves.

When Jesus interacted with people, He demonstrated the richness and abundance of God's love, which was a blend of both grace and truth. This kind of love wants the best for people, and it includes knowing when to give comfort and when to confront. Jesus was exquisitely tender with the poor, the sick, lepers, foreigners, misfits, and outcasts. The religious elite rejected these people, but Jesus welcomed them. Yet Jesus never said sin was acceptable. Sin crushes hearts and poisons minds, so Jesus spoke truth everywhere He went. It's fascinating that the arguments we see in the Gospels aren't between Jesus and the prostitutes, pimps, and thieves, but between Jesus and the self-righteous religious leaders. They were proud of following all the rules, but they missed God's heart.

What does it mean to love like Jesus?

- Those of us who have experienced the extraordinary love of God don't look the other way when people are hurting. We move toward them to provide comfort and care.

- Those of us who have experienced the extraordinary love of God don't stand back and condemn those who are radical sinners. We get to know them and earn the right to be heard.

- Those of us who have experienced the extraordinary love of God don't just tolerate those who have different views and assume all religions and philosophies are equal. We speak the truth, explaining God's truth with kindness and without condemnation.

- Those of us who have experienced the extraordinary love of God don't love only those who are easy to love. We dig deep to love those who are hard to love . . . people like you and me.

When people see this kind of love, they sit up and take notice.

True disciples are known by the depth of their love for people, especially for those who are different or difficult. Love is a clearer indication of devotion to Jesus than church attendance, proclamations of faith, Bible study, spiritual gifts, or service. Love is the most important trait of a disciple.

What kind of love? Genuine love, deep love, consistent love, sacrificial love. When people see this kind of love, they sit up and take notice. After the disciples had watched Jesus for three years, He announced, "Let me give you a new command: Love one another. In the same way I loved you, you love one another. This is how everyone will recognize that you are my disciples—when they see the love you have for each other" (John 13:34–35, MSG).

Those men surely thought, *I can't do that! I don't have the ability . . . or even the desire . . . to love people like you do!*

Great point, but God doesn't ask us to love others in our own strength and from our own resources. He gives us the limitless resources of His love to draw from. In John's first letter, he explained, "Dear friends, let us love one another, for love comes from God. Everyone who loves has been born of God and knows God. Whoever does not love does not know God, because God is love. This is how God showed his love among us: He sent his one and only Son into the world that we might live through him" (1 John 4:7–9, NIV).

But John didn't stop there. We can only express God's love to others to the extent we've experienced it ourselves. John tells us, "This is love: not that we loved God, but that he loved us and sent his Son as an atoning sacrifice for our sins. Dear friends, since God so loved us, we also ought to love one another" (verses 10–11). Are you having a hard time loving someone? Then dive deeper into God's love for you.

One day as I was studying the subject of love, I read a passage written by the Apostle Paul to the Christians in Ephesus: "For this reason I bow my knees to the Father of our Lord Jesus Christ . . . that Christ may dwell in your hearts through faith; that you, being rooted and grounded in love, may be able to comprehend with all the saints what is the width and length and depth and height—to know the love of Christ which passes knowledge; that you may be filled with all the fullness of God" (Ephesians 3:14, 17–19).

As I was meditating on this passage, I sensed God saying that there are many different ways people express love, but there are four distinct ways Jesus expressed love. In fact, He took love to entirely different dimensions. I like to call it "the four dimensions of the love of God." When we make it a goal to live in these four dimensions, we start looking more like Jesus, and we grow from a believer into a disciple.

FOUR DIMENSIONS OF LOVE

It's easy to love some people, but the real measure of a disciple is our love for the least, the lost, those from a different culture, and enemies. Let's look at what it means to love these people.

Loving the least

Caring for the poor is a theme that runs throughout Scripture. In fact, it's one of the dominant threads in the Bible. In one of His last messages, Jesus gave us a picture of the day of judgment. The unrighteous are those who don't care about the sick and needy, but the righteous notice and reach out to help. In the scene Jesus describes, the king commends the righteous for caring for those in need, but they're surprised by His praise.

> "Then the righteous will answer Him, saying, 'Lord, when did we see You hungry and feed You, or thirsty and give You drink? When did we see You a stranger and take You in, or naked and clothe You? Or when did we see You sick, or in prison, and come to You?' And the King will answer and say to them, 'Assuredly, I say to you, inasmuch as you did it to one of the least of these My brethren, you did it to Me.'" (Matthew 25:37–40)

Soon after I began serving at the church in Richmond, I was introduced to a ministry that served homeless people in the city. One Saturday night I met with a few of the men on the street, but I quickly realized they were trying to rob me. I immediately knew I needed to get out of there!

I went back to my apartment and began to pray for the men. The next night Colleen came over to my apartment after church, and we sat on our porch to enjoy the evening. Soon two intoxicated men came stumbling down the street. As they got closer, I realized they were two of the men I'd met the previous night. I walked into the street to talk to them. One of the men got angry and ran off, but the other stayed to talk. When it started raining, I invited him to sit on the porch with me. He told me his name was Cecil. As I explained the gospel to him, he understood and believed. When he trusted in Jesus, he instantly and supernaturally sobered up!

I was thrilled at the moment, but then I wondered what I was going to do with Cecil. I brought him into our apartment, fed him, let him take a shower, gave him some of my clothes, and provided a place for him to sleep until we could find a better home for him. Cecil had been an alcoholic for thirty-three years, so even though he was sober, he started experiencing severe withdrawal symptoms. The next day we found a rehab clinic where he could get the medical help he needed. When I left him there, I told him, "I'll come visit you every day until you complete this program, and then I'll help you find a better life."

I went to the clinic to see Cecil every day, either in the morning or the evening. In about two weeks, he had detoxed and had stabilized, so the clinic discharged him. He began going to church with Colleen and me, and some of his friends, the drunks and thieves, wanted to come, too. I loaded ten or twelve of them in a cargo van on Sunday morning and brought them to church. At the time, we only had about sixty people in the church, so our vanload of men significantly increased our attendance . . . even though the men frightened some of our regular attenders.

For the next year, I walked with Cecil through a process of discipleship. I helped him get a job, buy a car, and find a place to live, and he started serving as an usher in the church. His life had completely turned around.

Colleen and I planned to get married, but we had a problem. Colleen came from a Catholic background, and her family had withdrawn from her. They didn't plan to attend our wedding, so she had no one to walk her down the aisle. We asked Cecil, the formerly homeless alcoholic, to do the honors. That day he put on a tuxedo, put Colleen's arm in his, and walked her to the front of the church where I was waiting.

Our experience with Cecil opened doors for our church to care for other homeless people, immigrants, and others in need. I realized it's very easy to give a few dollars or even a few hours to people in need, but it's a very different thing to give them our hearts. Caring for them is almost always time consuming and messy. Quite often, they've gotten where they are by making many bad choices, or they're victims of others' horrible choices—and usually both. Either way, their lives need a lot of unraveling and reweaving. Ever since Colleen and I got married, we've made it a practice to be open to people in need. We often have people live in our home until they can get on their feet.

> I realized it's very easy to give a few dollars or even a few hours to people in need, but it's a very different thing to give them our hearts.

Those who live in the suburbs can easily lose connections with needy people. That's the reason they moved to the suburbs! But that's dangerous for a disciple of Jesus Christ. We need to do whatever it takes to stay connected to people who are less fortunate, who have lost hope, who have made terrible choices, or who are victims of abuse.

Some might ask, "Isn't it a risk for you and your family to have people living with you?" Yes, certainly. I can tell stories of some harrowing experiences with a few of the people we've brought to live with us. But I can also relate stories of how simple acts of kindness healed hearts, gave comfort, and provided a new start for people who had lost all hope for a better life. Through all those connections, our hearts have grown more sensitive to the needs of people around us.

One of the most gratifying experiences of being a disciple is helping people who can't give us anything in return. When we start loving like that, we're loving a little more like Jesus.

Loving the lost

At one point, a religious leader challenged Jesus to identify the single most important commandment in all the Old Testament. He had plenty to choose from! He replied, "'You shall love the Lord your God with all your heart, with all your soul, and with all your mind.' This is the first and great commandment. And the second is like it: 'You shall love your neighbor as yourself.' On these two commandments hang all the Law and the Prophets" (Matthew 22:37–40). Did you get that? Everything in the Bible is summarized and compacted into those two commands: Love God and love people.

Those who love God and others affect the lives of the people they meet every day. The love of God shines through them to reveal both darkness and light, and they are salt to flavor and preserve those whose lives were rotting in selfishness and despair. (We'll look more closely at the metaphors of light and salt in another chapter.) Conversely, the reason believers don't win many (or any) people to Christ is that their faith is just window dressing on their lives. They're not passionate about God or the things God cares about—and God cares about people. Believers are wrapped up in their own goals, their own convenience, and their own pleasures. Anyone who gets in the way of those things is a nuisance.

I've noticed that individuals who love the lost grow spiritually because they have to stay sharp to answer questions and engage people whose

I've noticed that individuals who love the lost grow spiritually because they have to stay sharp to answer questions and engage people whose lives are a mess (at least, below the surface).

lives are a mess (at least, below the surface). And I've noticed that the churches that love the lost grow numerically because they continually attract people who are desperate for forgiveness and hope.

All of us know people who are hard to love. Jesus knew plenty of them. When we read the Gospels, we see Him tenderly reaching out to touch lepers, treating prostitutes with respect, welcoming despised tax collectors (who collected money for the Roman occupiers), and befriending foreigners, children, and women—all of whom were considered second-class citizens. But we see Him in fierce confrontations with the religious leaders who oppressed the outcasts and misfits. I can imagine Jesus often shook His head when He finished conversations with those leaders.

One of the recent challenges in the church that has become a lightning rod of controversy is how Christians should respond to the cry in the LGBT community for equal rights and fair treatment. Many believers see the recent Supreme Court rulings on gay marriage as a disastrous historical moment of cultural collapse. As Christians have been asked to engage in this cultural shift, many unfortunately haven't done the best job representing Christ. Consequently, the church has been blamed for being judgmental and unloving. The clash of cultures has created a huge dilemma for Christians. The question we need to answer is: "How do I love people who think and live their sexuality in a different way than I believe the Bible teaches . . . without compromising either truth or love?"

Several years ago, I decided to make a special effort to improve the conversation with the gay community. As I got to know a number of those in the LGBT community, I saw many deep wounds they'd suffered because they'd been condemned by people in the church. I also soon realized the younger generation is much more accepting of gay people than older people. If the church continues to appear (and to be) harsh and judgmental toward gays, we run the risk of losing the entire generation of young people who leave the church to escape our rigid, fierce, narrow, unloving message toward gays.

The reality is that all people are born with sinful desires, and no matter the sin, all of us are helpless and hopeless apart from the redemptive grace of God. The sin of self-righteousness needs the forgiving touch of God just as much as adultery, robbery, drunkenness, homosexuality, and any other sin. When we're convinced that "the ground is level at the foot of the cross," we don't look down at anyone. We don't establish a dividing line of "acceptable sins" and "unacceptable sins." Because all of us are born with sinful desires, we all need to be "born again" as Jesus taught. When we're born again, we then receive the power—the Holy Spirit's power—to change any desire that doesn't align with God's will for our lives.

As someone moves from a believer to a disciple, one of the biggest signs of change is that the person begins to view others through the lens of God's love instead of judgment. When Jesus interacted with sinners, He didn't focus His attention on their sins. He touched them, healed them, picked up their babies, and had dinner with them—including prostitutes and tax collectors. Jesus loved them all, and He made sure they felt His love. He didn't see them as targets for evangelism; He saw them as objects of His love.

Quite often, the very best way to touch the heart of lost people is by serving them. Several years ago, Colleen and I moved into a new neighborhood. As we met our neighbors, we soon realized the couple next door wasn't married. When the young woman found out I was a pastor, she asked me to marry them. I said, "I'd be glad to, but first I'd like to meet with the two of you and talk about God's purpose for marriage." They agreed. As I explained God's design for their marriage, I told them God wanted them to be sexually pure before the wedding day. Since they'd been living together, the next best thing was for one of them to move out so they could remain chaste until the wedding. To my surprise, they agreed, so the guy temporarily moved in with his parents.

After their wedding, the couple wasn't attending a church. One Saturday as I prepared my sermon for the next day on evangelism, the Lord spoke to me: "I want you to do something to serve your neighbor next door. I want you to cut their grass."

I wasn't immediately thrilled and obedient. I complained, "But Lord, they have such a big yard! And I just have a little lawn mower that has a bag on the side. And besides that, it's fall, and there are tons of leaves on the ground. I'll have to stop every few feet to put the grass and leaves in a bag. This is going to take me forever!"

For some reason, God wasn't dissuaded by my reasonable objections. After a couple of minutes, I tried a different approach. I said, "Lord, I can't cut their grass because I'm working on my sermon."

He simply told me, "Dennis, this *is* your sermon."

I rolled the lawn mower out of my garage and started on my neighbor's yard. I could tell they weren't home, but I hoped they'd come while I was cutting their grass. They'd be so amazed at my humility and servanthood! After several hours, I was sweaty and tired. As I put the mower away, they still hadn't come home. I couldn't wait to see their car pull into the driveway so I could tell them I had cut their grass, but God whispered, "Don't tell them."

What? What's the use in serving if no one knows? I decided I wouldn't tell them until they asked.

A day went by, then a week, then a month, and then three months. They never asked if I had cut their grass! Every time I saw them, I tried to speak secret body language that said, "Yeah, it was me. I cut your grass!" But they never asked. Never.

After several months, the wife banged on our door one Saturday afternoon. She was frantic. She told us that her husband was throwing things in the house and was totally out of control. She said, "Dennis, can you calm him down long enough for me to grab my things so I can leave?"

Colleen assured her, "Dennis will help you."

Oh, great. Thanks. My own wife is volunteering me for a war zone.

I thought, *If he's that violent, why don't you call somebody else, like the SWAT team?* But the words that came out of my mouth were, "Sure. I'll go right now!"

When I opened the door and walked in, I didn't see him. I walked slowly through the house, and I finally found him on their bedroom floor. The room looked like a tornado had just hit it, and he didn't look any better. At first, he was furious at his wife, and he poured out his anger. But after a while, he began crying. He realized he was losing her because he couldn't control his temper. In the middle of this intense and heartbreaking conversation, he looked up at me and asked, "Did you cut my grass?"

I'm not kidding. That's what he said. I must have looked stunned because he asked again, "Dennis, did you cut my grass a few months ago?"

I nodded, and for the next half hour, he listened as I told him about the cleansing, healing power of Jesus' love. During perhaps the most traumatic day of his life, he remembered I had served him, and he was willing to listen to the message of hope. Right there in the chaos of his bedroom and his life, he trusted in Jesus.

That event happened twenty years ago. We don't live next to each other any longer, but I still go by to see him from time to time. Sometimes we look back on that time and laugh that it took him so long to ask me if I had cut his grass. It was a small thing for me to do, but it created an open door for a desperate man to listen when it was the right time for me to tell him about Jesus.

This is something I know about you: you can cut someone's grass, too. There's no telling how God will use a simple act of serving to touch a person's heart.

Loving across cultures

Currently, 140 nations are represented in the congregation of our church. Every gathering is like a meeting of the United Nations! Becoming an open, welcoming, inclusive church hasn't come quickly or easily, but it has happened.

Martin Luther King, Jr. once commented that the most segregated hour in American life is 11:00 on Sunday mornings. When I became a Christian, God began to do something in my heart about race relations— or more precisely, how I view people of other races. As I read the Bible, I saw that God doesn't love one race more than another, and He doesn't prefer one skin color over any others. Jesus died for all of us, and He wants us to love and accept each other regardless of race, ethnicity, color, or nationality.

Before Jesus ascended, He left instructions for His disciples: "But you shall receive power when the Holy Spirit has come upon you; and you shall be witnesses to Me in Jerusalem, and in all Judea and Samaria, and to the end of the earth" (Acts 1:8).

His followers were all Jewish, so we can imagine how they responded. Jerusalem? Check. No problem there. Judea? Good. These are still our people. But Samaria? Whoa, wait a minute! Those are half-breeds who have perverted God's truth! And the ends of the earth? Jesus, don't you understand that *we're* God's chosen people?

The disciples didn't have long to wonder how wide the gospel might reach. Ten days later, the Holy Spirit descended on the 120 who had been praying in the Upper Room. Luke tells us that people "from every nation under heaven" were in Jerusalem for the feast of Pentecost. When the Spirit came upon them, the disciples received the ability to speak in languages they had never learned. The crowds were astounded. They asked, "Look, are not all these who speak Galileans? And how is it that we hear, each in our own language in which we were born? Parthians and Medes and Elamites, those dwelling in Mesopotamia, Judea and Cappadocia, Pontus and Asia, Phrygia and Pamphylia, Egypt and the parts of Libya adjoining Cyrene, visitors from Rome, both Jews and proselytes, Cretans and Arabs—we hear them speaking in our own tongues the wonderful works of God" (Acts 2:7–11).

> **One of the great stains on today's church is our inability or unwillingness to gladly embrace people who are different from us.**

From the beginning, the gospel of Christ and the power of the Spirit broke down cultural barriers and created unity of heart and purpose. One of the great stains on today's church is our inability or unwillingness to gladly embrace people who are different from us. We've followed the example of the earthly kingdom instead of Christ and His heavenly kingdom. In the earthly culture, people are suspicious of any differences and they condemn anything that makes them feel uncomfortable. However, when we, as disciples, are committed to live according to God's heavenly culture, we respond quite differently:

- We value every person as Christ values them, as infinitely valuable.
- We go out of our way to connect with people who aren't like us.
- We give up our rights and our comfort so we can pursue a higher order of unity.
- We seek to understand rather than seeking to be understood.
- We determine to love people no matter how they treat us.

Just as the younger generation sees hypocrisy when we don't reach out to gay people, they see racism when our churches are predominately only one race, color, or culture.

When I served with the church in Richmond, we were lily white. One Sunday morning a black lady walked in with her three little daughters. They immediately realized few of us could keep the beat in the music, and our worship wasn't very expressive. I could tell this woman felt very uncomfortable, and I assumed her daughters did, too. I wondered why in the world they would come to our church when there are plenty of wonderful black churches in the city.

Colleen and I were dating at the time. After church, we invited them over to my apartment for lunch. Colleen cooked a nice meal, and we all sat down together. After a few minutes, this lady began to cry—not a sad cry, but a cleansing, healing cry. I asked her what was wrong, and she told me, "Dennis, this is the first time in my life that a white person has invited me into their home." She paused to wipe her eyes, and then she said, "I've worked for white people all my life, but nobody ever treated me as an equal . . . until today."

That moment changed me. I realized our society—and especially the Christian church—has a long way to go toward treating people with equality, justice, and genuine love. We started a friendship that day. The woman's daughters became like our daughters. Colleen and I babysat for her from time to time, and her middle daughter was a flower girl at our wedding. Eventually this beautiful woman became the worship leader at our church, and her presence attracted many people of color to attend, making it one of the first truly integrated churches in Richmond, Virginia. Her daughters grew up and formed a well-known Christian singing group called Out of Eden. They have had an impact for Jesus on thousands of people.

Over the years as we've watched our church in Atlanta reach across cultural barriers, we've seen people learn to love others in spite of their differences and exalt Christ's culture of love over their own earthly culture. Young people are watching the church to see how we respond. In this multi-cultural society, will we truly love people who are different from us, or will we erect barriers, showing that we're irrelevant, out of touch, and judgmental?

Loving enemies

Payback is deeply rooted in human nature. We don't have to teach our children to despise people who have hurt them; it comes naturally. Perhaps the highest order of love is the God-given capacity to love people who have made themselves our enemies. In Jesus' day, the rule of "an eye for an eye" was meant to keep quarrels from escalating: The law of reciprocity kept someone from gouging out two eyes in retaliation for losing one. But Jesus had a different plan. In His most famous sermon, He told the crowd:

> "You have heard that it was said, 'You shall love your neighbor and hate your enemy.' But I say to you, love your enemies, bless those who curse you, do good to those who hate you, and pray for those who spitefully use you and persecute you, that you may be sons of your Father in heaven; for He makes His sun rise on the evil and on the good, and sends rain on the just and on the unjust. For if you love those who love you, what reward have you? Do not even the tax collectors do the same? And if you greet your brethren only, what do you do more than others? Do not even the tax collectors do so? Therefore you shall be perfect, just as your Father in heaven is perfect." (Matthew 5:43–48)

This was a revolutionary teaching . . . and to many who heard Him, absurd! Who in the world loves those who have deliberately harmed them and who want to inflict additional harm? Most of the problems that keep us up at night are directly or indirectly tied to strained relationships.

Who are our enemies? Sometimes they are family members who have abandoned us or abused us, sometimes they are friends who have let us down, sometimes they are bosses who demand too much or coworkers who don't pull their load, and sometimes they are people who hold political views that are the opposite of ours—and we can't stand it!

Let me be clear: Loving our enemies doesn't mean we foolishly expose ourselves to harm, and it doesn't mean we have to trust untrustworthy people, but it certainly means we want the best for every person we know. We don't wish them harm, and we don't look for ways to make them pay for what they've done to us. We have to dive deep into the grace of God to find more love, forgiveness, and power than ever before. If our spiritual tank isn't full and overflowing, we won't have the ability to love those who have offended us.

In Paul's letter to the Romans, he didn't sugarcoat the difficulties of loving our enemies, but he didn't let us off the hook either. He wrote:

> Do not repay anyone evil for evil. Be careful to do what is right in the eyes of everyone. If it is possible, as far as it depends on you, live at peace with everyone. Do not take revenge, my dear friends, but leave room for God's wrath, for it is written: "It is mine to avenge; I will repay," says the Lord. On the contrary:
>
> "If your enemy is hungry, feed him;
>   if he is thirsty, give him something to drink.
> In doing this, you will heap burning coals on his head."
> Do not be overcome by evil, but overcome evil with good.
> (Romans 12:17–21, NIV)

It staggers me that as Jesus hung on the cross after being tortured by His enemies, He looked at those who despised Him and were murdering Him, and He prayed, "Father, forgive them for they don't know what they're doing." That's the epitome, the highest order of sacrificial love.

Forgiveness is an action that triggers a lot of memories. As you've read this chapter, what faces and events have come to mind? When we are offended and respond in fear by cowering or running away, or when we react in anger by trying to get even with the other person, we continue the cycle of harm and retribution. Only extraordinary love changes the script. The only way out of that cycle is for someone—for Christ's disciples—to forgive their enemies and love them enough to speak the truth and offer a way forward toward healing, hope, and reconciliation.

NEVER ALONE

When we try to demonstrate love in these four areas, we aren't on our own. Jesus loved the least—those people no one else even noticed. He loved the lost so much that He gave his life for all of us. He loved Jews, Samaritans, Greeks, and Romans—no race or nationality was beyond the scope of His affection. And Jesus loved His enemies. He died for the hardhearted, jealous religious leaders who killed Him, for those who didn't care about Him at all, and for all people everywhere. He loves the vicious and the pitiful, the distracted and the profane, the irreligious and the hyper-religious. Jesus didn't wait for people to come to Him. He took the initiative to reach out, to sacrifice His time and effort, and ultimately, to give everything He had.

> As His disciples, we follow Jesus' example, and we invite the Spirit of God to supernaturally produce this kind of love for others in us.

As His disciples, we follow Jesus' example, and we invite the Spirit of God to supernaturally produce this kind of love for others in us. When this happens, we don't love only those who love us . . . we love everybody.

THINK ABOUT IT:

1. Do you agree or disagree that the church has an image problem with people in our communities, many of whom see us as narrow, rigid, and judgmental? Why or why not?

2. Look at Paul's prayer in Ephesians 3:14–21. What do you think it means to "comprehend with all the saints what is the width and length and depth and height" of the love of Christ?

3. Who are some of "the least" in your community? What is one thing you can do in the next couple of days to reach out to them?

4. Why is it important to serve the lost as well as share the gospel with them? Why do some people feel attacked by zealous Christians? Have any of your friends or family members ever felt that way? Explain your answer.

5. When was the last time you invited someone from another culture into your home? When will be the next time (or the first time)?

6. You may not have any real enemies, but we all have people who annoy us. What needs to happen in your heart so you genuinely want the best for these people?

7. Rate yourself on a scale of 0 (zip) to 10 (a lot like Jesus) in your extraordinary love for people who aren't like you. Explain your rating. What needs to change in order to improve your score?

CHAPTER 3

A DISCIPLE HAS . . .
THE HEART OF A SERVANT

I'm a dreamer. I used to dream about being and doing something so magnificent that people would be amazed. In high school, I dreamed of being a star running back in the NFL, but that was shattered by the reality that I was too small and too slow. Later I hoped to build a fabulous company and make an incredible amount of money. That dream was on its way to being fulfilled . . . until I met Jesus. In the light of God's truth, it quickly became clear that my dreams had been self-focused. They were only about *my* success, *my* glory, and *my* pleasure.

For a while, I believed all ambition was evil, but that's not true. Paul wrote to the Corinthians, "Therefore we also have as our ambition . . . to be pleasing to Him" (2 Corinthians 5:9, NASB). I learned that ambition itself is not wrong; it's all about our purpose. The object of our ambition can be godly or ungodly. The closer I got to Jesus, the more I realized He measures greatness on a very different scale. Jesus turned everything I had thought about ambition, power, and success upside down.

THE SOURCE

In one of the most beautiful and stunning passages in the Bible, Paul gives us a new definition of greatness. First, he begins by reminding the Christians in Philippi that God has already filled them with His love, strength, and grace. He explains that this security and love radically changes how we relate to each other. He writes: "Therefore if you have any encouragement from being united with Christ, if any comfort from his love, if any common sharing in the Spirit, if any tenderness and compassion, then make my joy complete by being like-minded, having the same love, being one in spirit and of one mind. Do nothing out of selfish ambition or vain conceit. Rather, in humility value others above yourselves, not looking to your own interests but each of you to the interests of the others" (Philippians 2:1–4, NIV).

But Paul knew (and God knows) that selfless service runs counter to our human nature. We need more than a gentle reminder to let the love of God overflow in us and through us. We need a clear example to follow. Paul continues:

> In your relationships with one another, have the same mindset as Christ Jesus:
>
> Who, being in very nature God,
>> did not consider equality with God something to be used to
>> his own advantage;
> rather, he made himself nothing
>> by taking the very nature of a servant,
>> being made in human likeness.
> And being found in appearance as a man,
>> he humbled himself
>> by becoming obedient to death—
>> even death on a cross!
> Therefore God exalted him to the highest place
>> and gave him the name that is above every name,
> that at the name of Jesus every knee should bow,
>> in heaven and on earth and under the earth,
> and every tongue acknowledge that Jesus Christ is Lord,
>> to the glory of God the Father. (Philippians 2:5–11, NIV)

Don't miss this: Jesus had lived for all eternity in the incredible splendor of heaven. For uncounted centuries, the angels had sung His praises, and Jesus lived in perfect harmony with the Father and the Spirit. But because He loved us, He stepped out of heaven to become one of us, and even more, He "made himself nothing by taking the very nature of a servant." The King of glory was born in a stable, the Creator of all became vulnerable, the One who deserved all praise forfeited His security to give himself for us. He was willing to be misunderstood, mocked, despised, tortured, and killed . . . to serve you and me. The Lion of Judah was also the Lamb of God; the King of Glory "made himself nothing" to become the servant of all.

> **The point is crystal clear: we will serve others with humility and wisdom only to the extent we are amazed that Jesus has served us.**

The point is crystal clear: we will serve others with humility and wisdom only to the extent we are amazed that Jesus has served us.

CHOICES

Jesus' followers had a front row seat to observe Him for over three years, but instead of being amazed every day that the infinite Son of God came to serve, the Twelve didn't get it. They regularly saw Jesus stoop to care for people, yet they were driven by ambition. They were competitive and fearful they'd be left behind when Jesus established His new kingdom. Even during their final meal when Jesus tried to explain His imminent death to them one last time, they were distracted by their selfish pursuits. As Jesus told them He was going to give His life for them, they jockeyed for the highest positions in His cabinet. Who would be Secretary of State? Who would be in charge of the Treasury? Luke paints the scene for us:

Then they began to argue among themselves about who would be the greatest among them. Jesus told them, "In this world the kings and great men lord it over their people, yet they are called 'friends of the people.' But among you it will be different. Those who are the greatest among you should take the lowest rank, and the leader should be like a servant. Who is more important, the one who sits at the table or the one who serves? The one who sits at the table, of course. But not here! For I am among you as one who serves." (Luke 22:24–27, NLT)

Believers may sing praise songs and quote the Scriptures, but their hearts are still like the men sitting at the table with Jesus: they're driven by ambition to have more prestige, power, and possessions. Disciples are thrilled and amazed that Jesus has served them to the point of death on a cross, and they live by three principles of servanthood:

1. True greatness begins with a humble heart.

We've already received far more than we deserve. We were not created to be great ourselves, but to reflect the greatness of God. It's all about Him, not us.

2. A humble heart is formed by serving others.

Jesus, the Creator and King, stepped into the messy and broken lives of people over and over again to care for them. He was born in obscurity; His family had to become refugees in Egypt to escape death; when He was asked about the inscription on a coin, He had to borrow one; He rode into Jerusalem on a borrowed donkey's colt instead of a stallion; and He refused to call legions of angels for protection when the religious leaders had Him arrested. Even His most gracious actions were criticized.

During His final week, some people expected Jesus to proclaim himself a king who would kick the Romans out of the country, but Jesus was a very different kind of king—one who gave away power instead of demanding it. Jesus wasn't at all what they expected, but He was exactly what they desperately needed.

We may think that serving others will win approval and gratitude, but that's not always so. When Jesus healed people on the Sabbath, the religious leaders condemned Him instead of praising Him. The more He loved people, the more they hated Him . . . and eventually, they killed Him.

3. As we give ourselves away, we'll be fulfilled and secure.

This is the paradox of the Christian life: the more we give away, the more God fills us. As we give, love, and serve others, God does something in our hearts. He shines His light on our impure motives—not to blast us with condemnation, but to invite us to repent and experience His love even more. Gradually or quickly, we experience more of the presence of God. Our hearts are filled, and we're more secure, so we want to serve even more.

Today, people are obsessed with themselves. They post on Facebook and count the number of likes, they post on Twitter and see how many people are following them, and they take innumerable selfies to catalog every event in their lives. Being self-absorbed, though, isn't filling their emotional, spiritual, or relational tanks. People today are more depressed and lonely than ever.[3]

Paul reminded the Christians in Rome, "Focusing on the self is the opposite of focusing on God. Anyone completely absorbed in self ignores God, ends up thinking more about self than God. That person ignores who God is and what he is doing. And God isn't pleased at being ignored" (Romans 8:7–8, MSG).

A few years ago, I was asked to speak at a church in Florida. That morning the rain came down in buckets. When Colleen and I parked in the parking lot, a golf cart immediately arrived to pick us up. The driver was drenched, but he cheerfully invited us, "Hop in!" Colleen and I jumped in the cart. A couple of seconds later, I realized the driver was Mike Huckabee, the former Governor of Arkansas and recent candidate for President of the United States! We talked for the minute or so it took to get to the front door of the church, and he drove off to pick up more people. After the service, I had a chance for a longer conversation with him. I asked why someone of his stature and with his busy schedule was driving a golf cart in the church parking lot. He shrugged and said, "Dennis, I follow Jesus Christ. Jesus was always a humble servant, so if I follow Him, I want to serve, too." I said something about his candidacy, and he explained, "If I'm serious about being the leader of this nation, I need to be the chief servant."

DEVELOPING A SERVANT'S HEART

Some people might ask at this point, "Okay, I get it. But where do I start? What can I do?" We don't have to look far to see where we can serve. God has put each of us in a web of relationships, and he wants us to serve the people in that web, including our families, our communities, and our churches. We have dozens of choices each day to live for ourselves or to serve someone else. We can stop to listen instead of rushing off to the next thing on our to-do list, we can support someone else's idea that's close to the one we were going to propose, we can turn off the television to help with homework, we can wash the dishes instead of assuming someone else will do them, we can thank those who do big or little things that contribute to our happiness . . . the options are endless, if

Each opportunity to serve is a small death of our comfort and plans, but it leads to a deeper understanding, more affection, and stronger relationships—the abundant life.

we'll only notice. Each opportunity to serve is a small death of our comfort and plans, but it leads to a deeper understanding, more affection, and stronger relationships—the abundant life.

Serve people in your family.

We have the most opportunities to serve (and the most opportunities to be selfish) in our family relationships. Dozens of times a day, and in countless ways, we can "look out for the interests of others" instead of ourselves. If we do, the entire atmosphere in our homes might be radically transformed . . . for the better.

In two of Paul's letters, he gives instructions for households. In Ephesians, he gives the overarching concept: "Submit to one another out of reverence for Christ" (Ephesians 5:21, NIV). Humility isn't God's design for just the kids or one of the spouses, but for everybody. We are to be so amazed with the greatness and grace of God that we treat each other with the ultimate respect.

Wives are to respect their husbands in the same way they respect Christ. And husbands are to love their wives with the same kind of sacrificial devotion Jesus demonstrated when he gave His life for us. When couples are trying to live this way under the loving leadership of Jesus, they talk and listen, they find common ground instead of living with suspicion and resentment, and they provide a hothouse of growth for their kids.

I've never seen a couple devoted to serving each other who had a bad marriage. It won't happen. Oh, there will be plenty of disagreements and hurts to resolve, but they won't be demanding and bitter—two traits that ruin marriages. If one or both spouses insist on being served, strains inevitably occur in the fabric of the relationship, and the kids see a poor example of what marriage should be.

The closeness, vulnerability, and expectations in marriage reveal volumes about what's really in our hearts. We find out pretty quickly if we're selfish or servants. Let's be honest: all of us are selfish, and we need the Spirit's transforming love and power to turn us into servants. Marriage is a powerful classroom where we learn those crucial lessons.

One of the reasons many people avoid marriage today is because it immediately puts them in a place where they need to serve someone else . . . or the relationship starts to fall apart. I encourage single people to learn how to serve a roommate. I had many roommates before Colleen and I got married, and I can tell you that serving them wasn't my top priority! In fact, many of my roommate problems started with both of us taking more than giving. Sharing an apartment with someone can be a great training ground to develop a servant's heart! No matter what our living situation may be, we have the daily choice to humbly serve or to demand to be served.

Serve people in your community.

Today, we have the most advanced communication tools imaginable, but many of us don't even know our neighbors. We go to work, to school, or to the mall, and we come home without connecting with the people down the street or next door. Believers want to protect their privacy and their time, but disciples understand that God has put them in relationships for a reason. They are more concerned about the needs of others than their own convenience.

The Corinthians were having trouble being disciples. They were selfish, angry, and contentious. To give them an example of being a humble servant, Paul used his own experience:

> Even though I am free of the demands and expectations of everyone, I have voluntarily become a servant to any and all in order to reach a wide range of people: religious, nonreligious, meticulous moralists, loose-living immoralists, the defeated, the demoralized—whoever. I didn't take on their way of life. I kept

my bearings in Christ—but I entered their world and tried to experience things from their point of view. I've become just about every sort of servant there is in my attempts to lead those I meet into a God-saved life. I did all this because of the Message. I didn't just want to talk about it; I wanted to be *in* on it! (1 Corinthians 9:19–23, MSG)

Do we use our busyness as an excuse to avoid serving others? Paul was eager to take the gospel to the entire Roman world! Are we committed to our own priorities? Paul aligned his priorities with God's. Are there difficult people who are hard for us to love and serve? Paul waded in to love the jealous Corinthians, the arrogant Athenians, and the brutal Romans. In every encounter, he was determined to be the hands, feet, voice, and heart of Jesus to each person.

Who are the people in our communities? Many of us can list a boss, employees, and/or coworkers. Instead of doing as little as possible or being demanding (depending on our position), we're committed to others' success, their development, and their fulfillment. We take care to notice how they're doing, we ask good questions, and we really listen when they answer. We're quick to give credit to others when things go well, and we're willing to take our share of the blame when mistakes are made. We represent Christ as we get our work done.

The same principles are true at school, in neighborhoods, and in organizations. We don't participate to get, but to give. We help those who might be struggling with homework, we offer to water the plants while neighbors are out of town, and we enter into people's lives to notice and meet their needs. Will people notice? Some will, but some won't. And even those who see what we're doing may wonder about our motives. We can only change their cynicism into trust if we're consistent and kind.

Several years ago, I lived near a man who sat in a chair outside his open garage every afternoon as people came home from work. He kept several chairs on the driveway to encourage others to sit with him and visit for a while. He was a warm and talkative guy, and everybody loved him. He was a professional landscaper, and I'll never forget one winter when Atlanta had one of those awful ice storms that devastate tree limbs and make driving hazardous. This man and his crew went from house to house in the neighborhood to rescue trees by using ropes and stakes to pull them upright and stabilize them.

One of the big cedar trees in our yard was bent all the way to the ground. It looked more like a zero than an "I"! As soon as my neighbor saw my tree, he and his men came over to save it without even being asked. He just took the initiative to use his resources to serve his neighbors. While the rest of us were worried about keeping the power on and having enough food to last through the storm, this guy invested his resources to help others. Later I thanked him for saving my tree, and he just shrugged and explained, "One of the things that brings me joy is helping my neighbors."

The backstory to this account is fascinating: I had been ministering to the man for a couple of years, and I knew he was struggling with alcoholism. God was on the back burner of his life, yet he was still a much better model of service than many people I've known in the church. Because he was such a conscientious servant in the neighborhood, everybody loved hanging out at his house after work. He had influence that I didn't have because he served our neighbors better than I did. I realized if I was going to have more influence in my neighbors' lives, I was going to have to make time to serve them more. Serving others is probably the greatest tool to open the hearts of people to Jesus. How are you doing with that?

Serve in your church.

I believe there are three kinds of people who walk through the church doors: visitors, renters, and owners. Some people come just to check out the pastor, the music, the children's ministry, or some other aspect of the church. They may be back the next week, or they may visit another church. They're only *visiting*, so they don't have any inclination to serve. Another group of people who show up are *renters*. They come regularly, but they're consumers. They come as long as their needs are sufficiently met, but when they're not, they find somewhere else to go. It's like they're dancing with a partner, but they're always looking around to see if there's somebody better on the floor. To use another metaphor, renters treat the church like they're in a hotel room. They expect to get the benefits of comfort and convenience, but they don't make the bed and they leave the towels on the floor. Thankfully, other churchgoers are *owners*: they pray for the pastor and the ministries, tithe to the fund the operations, and devote their time and energy to serve others in the church.

All of us are in one of those three categories. Which represents your heart and your involvement?

God's design for the church is for every person to play an important role. Paul describes the church as "the body of Christ." Designated leaders—apostles, prophets, evangelists, pastors, and teachers—are to equip people to serve gladly and effectively. When the body is functioning properly, amazing things happen:

[We will] no longer be children, tossed to and fro and carried about with every wind of doctrine, by the trickery of men, in the cunning craftiness of deceitful plotting, but, speaking the truth in love, may grow up in all things into Him who is the head— Christ—from whom the whole body, joined and knit together by what every joint supplies, according to the effective working by which every part does its share, causes growth of the body for the edifying of itself in love. (Ephesians 4:14–16)

I remember the first time I studied this passage. I felt like God said to me, "Are you doing your share in the church to help it to grow?" I realized most of my life in the church had been spent just sitting in the audience, watching. I never considered my need to serve. But it was time. The next week Colleen and I walked up to the pastor of the new church we were attending, and I asked, "Where do you need someone to serve?"

I wasn't really prepared for his answer. He responded, "Well, Dennis, I need someone to clean the church between services. We don't have the money to hire anyone to do that yet."

I swallowed hard and asked, "Where else do you need someone to serve?"

He smiled and replied, "We also need someone to help us with the toddler ministry on Sunday nights. They're one- to five-year-olds." I looked at Colleen, hoping she would help me get out of this predicament, but instead she told him, "We'll serve in both of those areas!"

> I realized most of my life in the church had been spent just sitting in the audience, watching. I never considered my need to serve. But it was time.

We started our serving in two of the hardest areas of the church—hard for me, at least. Every Sunday night for a year, we taught the toddler ministry, and every Tuesday we came back to clean the church until they could afford to hire someone. When I look back on this experience, I realize it was the first test of faithfulness to see if we would serve in areas where we had no talent or desire. From that time on, we always had a ministry in the church, until the Lord called us away to Atlanta. I would soon realize this is one of the major differences between a believer and a disciple. I've never met a disciple of Jesus who wasn't a servant in the local church.

TAKING STOCK

Pride was Lucifer's sin when he declared in his defiant "I will" statements that he wanted to take God's place of glory and authority (see Isaiah 14:12–14). And pride has been the underlying sin of all humankind since the Garden when people, too, wanted to "be like God." Pride poisons hearts and ruins relationships as we are driven to be superior to others and hide our flaws to keep anyone from getting the upper hand. But arrogance doesn't always appear as supreme confidence. When we've concluded our best isn't good enough, we may slink into self-pity and even self-hatred. These traits, too, are evidence that we're trusting in our own efforts instead of God's grace—although our best efforts aren't good enough.

As we gain wisdom about humility and servanthood, we learn four very important realities:

1. In myself, I'm nothing. Paul wrote, "For if anyone thinks himself to be something, when he is nothing, he deceives himself" (Galatians 6:3). Apart from Christ, we are self-absorbed in our human relationships.

2. In myself, I know nothing. Paul explained, "And if anyone thinks that he knows anything, he knows nothing yet as he ought to know" (1 Corinthians 8:2).

3. In myself, I have nothing. In the same letter, Paul wrote, "For who makes you differ from another? And what do you have that you did not receive? Now if you did indeed receive it, why do you boast as if you had not received it?" (1 Corinthians 4:7)

4. In myself, I can do nothing. Jesus told us, "I am the vine, you are the branches. He who abides in Me, and I in him, bears much fruit; for without Me you can do nothing" (John 15:5).

But in Christ, the opposite is true:

1. I'm the righteousness of God in Christ Jesus
    (2 Corinthians 5:21).

2. I have the mind of Christ (1 Corinthians 2:16).

3. I have all things that pertain to life and godliness (2 Peter 1:3).

4. And I can do all things through Christ who gives me strength
    (Philippians 4:13; John 15:4).

To live in this new reality, we have to come to a place of nothingness in ourselves (that's humility), and then take on the life of a servant (that's like Jesus). As disciples, we live with the questions: "Where can I serve my family and friends? Where can I serve in my community? Where can I serve in my church?"

When serving starts to become a way of life for you, you are looking more and more like a disciple of Christ!

THINK ABOUT IT:

1. Who do you know who best exemplifies a servant's heart, someone who is more dedicated to the interests of others than his or her own interests? What impact does this person have on others? Is that lifestyle attractive to you? Why or why not?

2. Describe the ways Jesus has served you. What was His attitude as He gave himself for you? Why is it important to focus on how He has served us?

3. What are two things you can do right away to serve people in your family (or your roommate)?

4. What are two things you can do to serve people at work, in your neighborhood, or in an organization? When will you begin doing them? What do you hope will happen? What do you expect to happen?

5. In the church, what are some differences between visitors and renters ... and between renters and owners? In which group are you? Explain your answer.

6. Explain the paradox of giving our lives away so God can fill them.

7. On a scale of 0 (none) to 10 (completely), rate yourself on having the heart of a servant. Explain your answer. What needs to change in order to improve your score?

CHAPTER 4

A DISCIPLE IS . . .
SENSITIVE AND SUBMITTED
TO THE HOLY SPIRIT

When we mention the role of the Holy Spirit, many believers struggle to comprehend who the third person of the Trinity really is! When I became a believer, I attended a church that talked very little about the Holy Spirit because He was such a controversial subject in the body of Christ. Many in the church have never experienced the fullness of the Spirit, and therefore, they miss out on one of the most critical aspects of following and yielding to the voice of God.

I like to say it this way: The most important message to the unbeliever is Jesus, and the most important message to the believer is the Holy Spirit. When you study the life of Jesus, you discover that His ministry didn't begin until He came back from the desert empowered by the Holy Spirit. Everything He did on the earth was under the anointing of the Holy Spirit, and He let all those who would listen know that they could do the same works if they learned to cooperate with this same Holy Spirit.

Shortly after I had given my heart to Christ, I was introduced to the Holy Spirit. A man walked up to me in a mall in Cherry Hill, New Jersey, where I was sitting reading the Bible. I know it sounds odd, but I was a bit of an unusual Christian who was hungering to understand God so much that I read my Bible even in public places. As the man came up to me, he asked a startling question, "Have you received the Holy Spirit since you believed in Jesus?"

To be honest, I didn't know what to say at the moment. I told him I was a new believer and didn't know much about anything in the Bible, so that's why I was reading it. I explained that I grew up in a church that didn't really talk that much about the Holy Spirit, therefore, I wasn't sure who He was!

He told me to turn in my Bible to Acts 19 and read the first few verses. As I read it, I was amazed that this passage of Scripture perfectly described what I was experiencing right there. I read:

And it happened, while Apollos was at Corinth, that Paul, having passed through the upper regions, came to Ephesus. And finding some disciples he said to them, "Did you receive the Holy Spirit when you believed?"

So they said to him, "We have not so much as heard whether there is a Holy Spirit."

And he said to them, "Into what then were you baptized?"

So they said, "Into John's baptism."

Then Paul said, "John indeed baptized with a baptism of repentance, saying to the people that they should believe on Him who would come after him, that is, on Christ Jesus."

When they heard this, they were baptized in the name of the Lord Jesus. And when Paul had laid hands on them, the Holy Spirit came upon them, and they spoke with tongues and prophesied. (Acts 19:1–6)

After I read these verses, he asked, "Do you want to receive the Holy Spirit in the same way the men did in the Bible?"

At first I was a bit scared because it was so new to me, and I wasn't sure what would happen, but for some reason I responded, "I want everything God wants me to have, even if I don't understand it all!"

I asked him if we could go somewhere less public, so we went back to my hotel room. There he prayed for me to receive the Holy Spirit in a fresh new way. What happened to me after that was nothing short of supernatural! I began to experience the presence of God like I'd never experienced before. Shortly afterward, I began to pray in a new language that didn't make sense to my natural mind, but I would later learn that this is what happened to all the disciples in the Bible when they were filled with the Holy Spirit. At the time, I thought this was the most amazing thing I'd ever experienced outside of receiving Christ, but later I learned that not everyone in the body of Christ believes in this experience. The supernatural filling of the Spirit might be controversial for some, but I can't leave this experience out. It was the key to unlock what it means to be submitted to Christ and follow the voice of God.

> One of the most important differences between a believer and a disciple is how the person hears God and learns to follow His voice as He directs their lives.

The Bible tells us there are many roles the Holy Spirit plays in our lives when we learn to cooperate with Him, but perhaps none is more important than the fact that He is the voice of God who guides us in our journey as we move deeper into our relationship with Him. One of the most important differences between a believer and a disciple is how the person hears God and learns to follow His voice as He directs their lives.

OUR RELATIONSHIP WITH GOD DEPENDS ON THE HOLY SPIRIT

When Jesus ascended to the right hand of the Father, He didn't leave us as orphans. He explained to his disciples (including us) that He was sending the Holy Spirit to guide us, teach us, and empower us. We won't love Jesus unless the Holy Spirit shows us how much Jesus loves us, and we won't obey Him unless the Spirit convinces us that obeying God is more valuable than following our own desires. Jesus explained, "If you love Me, keep My commandments. And I will pray the Father, and He will give you another Helper, that He may abide with you forever—the Spirit of truth, whom the world cannot receive, because it neither sees Him nor knows Him; but you know Him, for He dwells with you and will be in you" (John 14:15–17). Some translations say Jesus will send an "advocate," and others call Him the "counselor" or the "comforter." But the Holy Spirit isn't a quilt! He is more like an attorney who defends us, protects us, and represents us. Because of the presence of the Spirit, we're never alone, never defenseless, and never powerless. How does the Holy Spirit deepen our relationship with God?

He reveals the nature and wonder of God.

I've heard a lot of people respond to the teaching of the Bible by grumbling, "That just doesn't make sense." Throughout history, unbelieving philosophers and teachers have tried to destroy the faith of millions. They use a myriad of "rational" arguments to ridicule the teaching of Jesus and the Bible, but they fail to understand that God's truth only makes sense to those whose minds and hearts have been enlightened by the Holy Spirit. The Corinthians had displayed an alarming level of selfishness and spiritual blindness, so Paul set them straight:

> However, we speak wisdom among those who are mature, yet
> not the wisdom of this age, nor of the rulers of this age, who are

coming to nothing. But we speak the wisdom of God in a mystery, the hidden wisdom which God ordained before the ages for our glory, which none of the rulers of this age knew; for had they known, they would not have crucified the Lord of glory.

But as it is written:

"Eye has not seen, nor ear heard,
Nor have entered into the heart of man
The things which God has prepared for those who love Him."

But God has revealed them to us through His Spirit. For the Spirit searches all things, yes, the deep things of God. For what man knows the things of a man except the spirit of the man which is in him? Even so no one knows the things of God except the Spirit of God. Now we have received, not the spirit of the world, but the Spirit who is from God, that we might know the things that have been freely given to us by God. These things we also speak, not in words which man's wisdom teaches but which the Holy Spirit teaches, comparing spiritual things with spiritual. But the natural man does not receive the things of the Spirit of God, for they are foolishness to him; nor can he know them, because they are spiritually discerned. (1 Corinthians 2:6–14)

The natural mind doesn't understand *grace*—we insist on earning God's love and acceptance. The natural mind doesn't trust God's *truth*— we insist we know more than God. And the natural mind doesn't depend on God's *power*—we believe we're self-sufficient. Disciples develop spiritual sensitivity to the revealed truth of God. Oh, they have plenty of questions, but they look to God and His Word for answers. The natural man doesn't understand the supernatural. Only by the Holy Spirit can we begin to cooperate with the supernatural side of God.

The Holy Spirit is the voice of God.

We need to be careful here. I've heard people over and over again insist, "God told me" when they want to do this or that. People have told me God told them to get married, and a couple of years later they said God told them to get a divorce. And many others have tried to impress people with their intimate connection with God by claiming He clearly spoke directly to them. Does God speak to us? Indeed, He does.

God speaks most clearly and consistently through the truth of His Word. Jesus is called the Word, and the Bible is called the Word. Both are voices God uses to speak His truth to us. In a heated argument with religious leaders who questioned Jesus' authority, He told them, "And if anyone hears My words and does not believe, I do not judge him; for I did not come to judge the world but to save the world. He who rejects Me, and does not receive My words, has that which judges him—the word that I have spoken will judge him in the last day. For I have not spoken on My own authority; but the Father who sent Me gave Me a command, what I should say and what I should speak. And I know that His command is everlasting life. Therefore, whatever I speak, just as the Father has told Me, so I speak" (John 12:47–50). And Paul explained how God speaks through the Bible: "All Scripture is given by inspiration of God, and is profitable for doctrine, for reproof, for correction, for instruction in righteousness, that the man of God may be complete, thoroughly equipped for every good work" (2 Timothy 3:16–17).

But we have a relationship with a person, not just a Book. The Holy Spirit communicates with us through an *inward witness* and an *inward voice*. Paul told the Romans, "The Spirit himself bears witness with our spirit that we are children of God" (Romans 8:16, ESV).

The enemy of our souls uses many tricks to get us off track in our walks with God. He often uses temptation, deception, and accusation. Sometimes a thought may rush into our minds that sneers, "How can you even call yourself a Christian? God can't forgive that!" Early in our Christian lives, especially, we can wonder if we belong to God at all. The Holy Spirit knows our weaknesses and fears, and He whispers (He "bears witness") to our hearts that the grace of God covers all our sins. (Even some of us older Christians need an occasional reminder that God delights in us as His children!)

The Spirit also speaks to us in an inward voice—not an audible one, but a voice that is unmistakable. We may have a question about a direction in our careers, or we may have struggles with family members or health or anything else. As we quiet our hearts and pray, sometimes the Spirit reminds us of a passage of Scripture to comfort and guide us, but other times we sense a message directly from the heart of God.

> The Spirit also speaks to us in an inward voice—not an audible one, but a voice that is unmistakable.

At a time of great heartache for the people of God, Isaiah assured them:

> "Your ears shall hear a word behind you, saying,
> 'This is the way, walk in it,'
> Whenever you turn to the right hand
> Or whenever you turn to the left."
> (Isaiah 30:21)

Let me be honest: There are plenty of times I sense the inward voice of God, but I don't listen. I may be talking to a person about a particular problem when the Lord whispers to me to say something, but I say something else. Or He tells me to keep quiet and listen, but I blurt out my opinion. I've learned there are three people in every conversation: the other person, me, and the Holy Spirit. I need to pay attention to both of the others who are present!

Thankfully, though, I've listened at least a few times. One of the most important moments of my experience of the Holy Spirit occurred when Colleen and I were finishing our ministry education in Tulsa, Oklahoma. We were trying to hear from God about our next move in ministry. We were both 31 at the time, and we knew God was calling us to plant a church in the Atlanta area, but we weren't sure exactly where to go.

After visiting our family just before graduation, we decided to drive around the perimeter of Atlanta on I-285. As we got to a portion of the expressway called "Spaghetti Junction" in the southern part of Gwinnett County, I sensed the Holy Spirit saying, "This is the area where you are to plant the church." I looked over at Colleen and could see she was experiencing something similar, so we pulled over and talked excitedly about what we sensed we were hearing God say. Neither of us had ever spent any time in this part of the city, and we knew absolutely nobody in the area. We bought a map of the city, went home, unfolded it, and placed a star on the spot where we felt God spoke to us.

For the next few months, we prayed over this area and asked God to help us understand what kind of church He wanted us to plant in that part of Atlanta. This is where it gets interesting: God immediately started speaking to us about having a church with over 100 nations in it. It seemed most unusual at the time because in 1990 Gwinnett county was eighty-five percent white, and only a few people from other nations lived anywhere nearby. Yet we started the church in response to the prompting of the Holy Spirit. A few years later the Olympics were held in Atlanta, and people from all over the world moved there. Of all places, the very spot where we started our church became a melting pot of nationalities! Today, after becoming a church of over 140 nations, we realize God wanted to demonstrate to the world how Christ breaks down the walls that separate us in society and show the world the power of His kingdom's culture over our earthly culture.

In the middle of our worship services, I often find myself thinking how important it is to be sensitive and submitted to the Holy Spirit when He speaks. I wonder what would have happened if Colleen and I hadn't listened to the Spirit and had just planted a church where we wanted to live. All the different nationalities worshiping together, all the mission projects we began around the world, all the churches around the nation that have seen our model and followed it—none of that would have happened! The difference between a believer and a disciple is how connected the person is to the Holy Spirit.

The Holy Spirit communicates truth.

In His long conversation with the disciples between their last meal together and His arrest, Jesus told them clearly about the role of the Holy Spirit. They were alarmed that He was going away (even though He had told them many times that He was going to be killed and then rise from the dead), but He assured them that the Holy Spirit would be with them: "And when He has come, He will convict the world of sin, and of righteousness, and of judgment: of sin, because they do not believe in Me; of righteousness, because I go to My Father and you see Me no more; of judgment, because the ruler of this world is judged" (John 16:8–11).

To show us our need for a Savior, the Holy Spirit shines His light on the darkness of our hearts. Similarly, to show Christians where we're out of step with God, He shines His light on our selfishness and sin. We shouldn't be surprised when the Spirit points out sin in our lives. "And there is no creature hidden from His sight, but all things are naked and open to the eyes of Him to whom we must give account" (Hebrews 4:13). He invites us to repent and trust in the love and grace of God once more.

The Spirit convicts us of righteousness—not ours, but Christ's. One of the amazing truths of the Bible is that when we trust in Jesus, His righteousness is credited to our account. It's "the great swap": He takes our sin, and we receive His righteous standing before God (2 Corinthians 5:21).

The Holy Spirit also convicts us of judgment. This isn't judgment against *us*, but against Satan, the ruler of the world. Earlier in this conversation, Jesus had told His followers, "Now is the judgment of this world; now the ruler of this world will be cast out" (John 12:31). This means that the death of Jesus has already won the victory over the evil one and his demons. The ruler of the world has no more authority over you and me.

The Spirit of God communicates God's truth to assure us that God is both good and great, and that we can trust Him with everything that happens in our lives.

THE HOLY SPIRIT IS THE POWER OF GOD

Many Christians just go through the motions. Their lives are no different from the agnostic's down the street. They go to church a couple of times a month, and they give a little when it's convenient. They pray when they're in trouble, but they seldom talk about God—unless they're really angry! To them, the power of the Holy Spirit is as foreign as the South Pole.

Disciples depend on the power of the Spirit for everything. This isn't a new or bizarre concept. Jesus told His followers, "But you shall receive power when the Holy Spirit has come upon you" (Acts 1:8). Paul explained, "My speech and my preaching were not with persuasive words of human wisdom, but in demonstration of the Spirit and of power, that your faith should not be in the wisdom of men but in the power of God" (1 Corinthians 2:4–5). And astoundingly, Jesus promised, "Most assuredly, I say to you, he who believes in Me, the works that I do he will do also; and greater works than these he will do, because I go to My Father. And whatever you ask in My name, that I will do, that the Father may be glorified in the Son. If you ask anything in My name, I will do it" (John 14:12–14).

These Scriptures have always challenged me. When you read them, you realize God has used people to accomplish seemingly impossible things through the power of the Holy Spirit. However, many Christians assume: That was then; this is now. They don't believe God will do supernatural things through them today. But as I read the Scriptures, I can't see anywhere that God decided to stop functioning supernaturally through people! The problem with many of us is that we attempt to make the supernatural fit into our natural thinking, which is why so many well-meaning believers never experience the incredible power of the Holy Spirit using them to do something supernatural. As people move from believers to disciples, they begin to ask God to use them as He used Jesus' disciples to heal sick people or cast out demons. The question is simple, but searching: Do you believe that God still does things like this today? And a second question is: Do you believe God wants to use you in this way as you learn to cooperate with the Holy Spirit?

WE WILL NEVER BE DISCIPLES UNTIL WE'RE FILLED WITH THE HOLY SPIRIT.

Something always is the dominant, controlling power in our lives. It may be money, alcohol, approval, success, possessions, or fame. Such things, we're sure, will fill our lives with joy and meaning, but they always fail to satisfy us. When we keep trusting them, we're foolish. Instead, Paul tells us to choose another dominant, controlling power to fill us—one that leads to real joy, real meaning, and real love—the power of the Holy Spirit. In his expansive and beautiful letter to the church in Ephesus, Paul instructed, "Do not be unwise, but understand what the will of the Lord is. And do not be drunk with wine, in which is dissipation; but be filled with the Spirit" (Ephesians 5:17–18).

What does the filling of the Spirit look like? In his letters, Paul provides some parallel thoughts. A couple of chapters earlier in the letter to the Ephesians, he prayed that we would "know the love of Christ which passes knowledge; that you may be filled with all the fullness of God" (Ephesians 3:19). And in his letter to the Colossians, he says the presence and power of the Spirit produce God's peace even when things are falling apart around us, and the Spirit illuminates the wonder of the Word: "Let the peace of God rule in your hearts, to which also you were called in one body; and be thankful. Let the word of Christ dwell in you richly in all wisdom" (Colossians 3:15–16).

Isn't this the life you've always wanted?

Isn't this the life you've always wanted? It's open and available to anyone who is willing to take it. The filling of the Spirit transforms our lives, but as an old pastor once said, "The problem is, I leak." Paul's encouragement isn't to be filled one time with the Spirit, but to be continually filled, to have such a strong dependence on God that the Spirit always supplies assurance, power, joy, love, and wisdom.

EVEN MORE

And the Spirit wants to do even more in and through us. The Bible teaches that we can be baptized in the Holy Spirit. It happened to the 120 disciples on the day of Pentecost when the Holy Spirit came upon them. Tongues of fire touched each one and they went out to proclaim the gospel of grace in the languages of the people from all over the world—languages the disciples had never learned, yet spoke with clarity and power. When we are baptized in the Spirit, God gives us a new language, one that enables our spirits to connect even more deeply with Him.

People receive this baptism in many different ways. When the man approached me in the mall and we talked about the Spirit, he asked if I wanted to be baptized in the Spirit. I was reluctant. I said, "Not here. Not in the mall!" I invited him to my hotel room, and he prayed for me there. Instantly, I sensed the presence of God more powerfully than I had ever imagined, and I began to speak in tongues. Some have this experience at the altar in church, some in their homes, and some in small groups. There's no right or wrong place for God to work powerfully in our lives in this way—any place will do!

WHAT CAN YOU EXPECT?

Some people are determined to prove they're good enough to go to heaven, and they insist on trusting in their own limited resources. Many others simply aren't aware God has given them the magnificent gift of the Holy Spirit to equip them, inspire them, and empower them. Still others resist the power of the Spirit because they're afraid He will make them say or do strange things, and they can't have that!

Let me assure you, you can trust the Holy Spirit. When you're filled with the Spirit, you'll experience more peace and patience, and you'll be more thankful because you'll realize God has poured himself out for you and in you. You'll have the power to love the unlovely, and you'll care for the lost and the least. You'll long to know God more intimately, and you'll make Him your highest priority. He'll become your everything!

As we walk in the Spirit, we'll trust God to change us—our hearts, our attitudes, and our actions. Paul called the result of this change "the fruit of the Spirit": love, joy, peace, patience, kindness, goodness, faithfulness, gentleness, and self-control (Galatians 5:22–23). Like fruit that grows on a tree, spiritual fruit grows slowly, from a nourishing source, in season, and beautifully. That fruit is for all Christians, but God also gives special abilities, called "spiritual gifts," to each individual to build up the body of Christ.

Spiritual gifts are listed in four places in the New Testament. The lists vary, which may indicate they aren't exhaustive. The point is that the Spirit empowers each of us to accomplish something wonderful and unique in the purposes of God. None of us is expendable. All of us matter, and God counts on all of us to use our gifts to touch people and honor Him. Spiritual fruit and spiritual gifts are evidence of the Holy Spirit dwelling *within* us, but the Bible also talks about the Holy Spirit coming *upon* people.

When the Holy Spirit comes upon you with power, you'll see and do things you never dreamed possible. God may give you prophetic utterances; sick people will be healed; demons will flee at your command; and you'll communicate with the heart of God through your own prayer language. You'll become wiser, kinder, and more loving than ever. Will you experience spiritual conflict? You bet, but you won't be afraid of people who oppose you, and you won't demand they agree with you. You'll love them . . . you'll be a little more like Jesus.

KEEP IN STEP WITH THE SPIRIT

As you've read this chapter, has the description of the power and presence of the Holy Spirit bored you, or does it awaken a deep longing in your heart? If you've read this far in the book, I would imagine the answer is B. You want more of the fullness of God. I've discovered three essential qualities all disciples need as they become more sensitive and submissive to the Holy Spirit.

Humility

James reminds us: "God opposes the proud but gives grace to the humble" (James 4:6, ESV). When we are full of ourselves, God can't fill us with the Holy Spirit. We must acknowledge our emptiness, and then we can come to God with open hands and expectant hearts. John the Baptist said, "He must increase, but I must decrease" (John 3:30). For the Spirit to have His way in us, we have to give Him room. That's why we fast, pray, and empty ourselves. As we've seen, without God we're nothing, but in Him, we have the fullness of the Spirit.

Pursuit

God is a gracious friend. He longs to be close to us, but He never forces himself on us. Yes, He pursued us first. We would have no hope without Him taking the initiative, but now, like any other true friendship, both parties take the initiative to reach out to each other. James gives us an invitation and a warning: "Draw near to God and He will draw near to you. Cleanse your hands, you sinners; and purify your hearts, you double-minded" (James 4:8).

The promise is that if we move toward God, He'll certainly move toward us. And He doesn't approach with a scowl or a wagging finger. When we think of "drawing near," it implies tenderness and kindness, like hugging someone we love. As we draw near to God, we're coming to the King of Glory, the One whose attributes are perfect and infinite, whom angels worship all day, every day. We shouldn't be surprised when, in contrast to His perfection, we notice the imperfections in ourselves. We realize that we've wanted two things: God *and* something else that promised fulfillment. But in the light of His love, wisdom, glory, and power, we repent of our double-minded thinking and pursue only Him.

Obedience

We can talk for hours about swimming, but we can't actually swim unless we get in the pool. Many Christians talk a good game about following Christ and being filled with the Spirit, but they stand on the sidelines. When God speaks, disciples act. Obedience isn't optional. Quite often, God tells us to do something we don't want to do, and it's hard to take that first step. We need to remember that Jesus obeyed the Father when it wasn't merely inconvenient; it cost Him His life. If He was willing to obey that much for us, surely we can suffer a little inconvenience for Him.

When God speaks, disciples act. Obedience isn't optional.

Many of us come up with a million excuses to delay our obedience: we have other priorities, the person won't understand or won't respond well, or it'll take too much time. There are a lot more, but you get the idea. Delayed obedience is disobedience. When God speaks and gives directions, it's time to take action. Of course, sometimes God builds a delay into His directions, like the time Colleen and I still had another year of Bible school when God told us to plant a church in Atlanta. But we were eager to obey as much as we could as soon as we could. That's the mark of a disciple.

The Christian life is an adventure, full of twists and turns. We have a leader who is far wiser than we are, far stronger, and far more loving. We can trust Him. The more we grasp the greatness and grace of God, the quicker we'll obey Him.

The Spirit-filled life is the only one worth living. Everything else is either boring, oppressive, or frightening. When we experience the presence and power of the Spirit, He doesn't magically cause all our problems to vanish. We still face obstacles. We still have heartaches. But we discover a connection with power and love unlike anything we've ever known. We don't just survive; we go deeper into the heart of God, experience more of Him than ever before, and become a beacon of hope for those around us.

That's what God wants for you and me. That's what I want, too. How about you?

THINK ABOUT IT:

1. What are some ways the Holy Spirit reveals the nature and purposes of God to us?

2. What are the ways God speaks to us? What are some specific instances when He has spoken to you? How did you respond? If you didn't respond in faith, how do you wish you had listened and acted?

3. What are some evidences of the Holy Spirit's power? Which have you experienced?

4. Describe what it means to be filled with the Spirit. What can we expect when we're filled?

5. Describe the baptism of the Spirit. What does God do in us and through us when we have this experience? Is this still available today? Is it something you want to experience? Why or why not?

6. Why are humility, pursuit, and obedience essential if we're to walk in the power of the Spirit?

7. On a scale of 0 (none) to 10 (absolutely), how sensitive and submitted are you to the Holy Spirit? Explain your answer. How might you improve your score?

CHAPTER 5

A DISCIPLE IS . . . GOVERNED BY THE AUTHORITY OF THE WORD

W e live in a world of communication that was unimaginable only a few years ago. We have virtually the entire scope of the world's knowledge instantly available in our pockets and purses, and we can connect with family, friends, and followers at any time about anything. This is one of the marvels of life in the information revolution. In seconds, we can find competing views on topics ranging from politics to recipes, dog training to psychology, lamps to landscaping.

The enormous wave of information is a tsunami that amazes us, but I'm not sure it has helped us grow in wisdom. Some people are a bit too naïve, assuming everything they read has been vetted and is true; others have been burned once too many times and have become skeptical. Actually, a lot of people who used to be naïve are now in the skeptical camp, and for good reason. It doesn't take too many "fake news" stories to make us wonder if what we're reading is trustworthy.

Being naïve, though, isn't a recently acquired trait of humanity. In the opening scenes of the Bible, the first couple had difficulty separating fact from fiction. God had given Adam and Eve a perfect environment and an intimate relationship with Him and each other. They had meaningful work, and they experienced complete fulfillment and joy. They were living in the literal Garden of Eden. God gave only one limiting command: "Of every tree of the garden you may freely eat; but of the tree of the knowledge of good and evil you shall not eat, for in the day that you eat of it you shall surely die" (Genesis 2:16–17).

Pretty clear, don't you think? Not ambiguous or complicated. As straightforward as it could be. Sometime later, the serpent, Satan, asked Eve a simple question: "Has God indeed said, 'You shall not eat of every tree of the garden'?"

Eve got a little confused. When she responded to the serpent's challenge, she failed to accurately quote God. She told Satan God had said, "We may eat the fruit of the trees of the garden; but of the fruit of the tree which is in the midst of the garden, God has said, 'You shall not eat it, nor shall you touch it, lest you die.'"

Taking advantage of Eve's lack of clarity, Satan sprang his trap. He insisted, "You will not surely die. For God knows that in the day you eat of it your eyes will be opened, and you will be like God, knowing good and evil" (Genesis 3:1–5).

Is this just an ancient story with little relevance to us today? No, it's as relevant as today's news. Satan's question to Eve is the same one implicitly asked by virtually every person on the planet: "Has God really said . . . ?" Even when God's commands are crystal clear, we—just like our ancestors in the Garden—rationalize, excuse, minimize, and deny that God gave us instructions at all.

This is one of the biggest differences between believers and disciples. Believers attend church, read their Bibles occasionally, and pray. They go to Bible studies and concerts, and they appear to be devoted followers . . . until God's commands conflict with their goals of happiness and prosperity. They don't expect God to ever contradict them, make them uncomfortable, or challenge their life's goals. When those things happen—and they certainly do because God is perfect in wisdom and power and we're, well, not—they shrug and find an excuse to ignore God.

Disciples have a very different response to God's Word. They see the truth of the Bible as God's sovereign and perfect message to them—even when it makes them uncomfortable. In fact, disciples expect God to contradict them and challenge their goals and values.

> Disciples have a very different response to God's Word. They see the truth of the Bible as God's sovereign and perfect message to them—even when it makes them uncomfortable.

When Paul wrote his first letter to the Christians in Thessalonica, he marveled at their trust in God's Word. He praised them: "For this reason we also thank God without ceasing, because when you received the word of God which you heard from us, you welcomed it not as the word of men, but as it is in truth, the word of God, which also effectively works in you who believe" (1 Thessalonians 2:13, NIV). They were disciples.

NECESSARY QUESTIONS

When I trusted in Christ and began to walk with God, I noticed that God's will and ways are far different from the way I'd been living. My deeply ingrained thought patterns and behaviors weren't consistent with what I was reading about God's will in the Bible. I asked myself some probing questions, and I believe all who desire to be disciples ask these questions at some point.

- Do I believe the Bible is the true Word of God?

- Do I want the Bible to be the standard of truth for how I live my life, or is there some other standard worthy of my allegiance?

- How will I respond when my goals and desires conflict with what the Word says?

- Do I really believe that living by the Word of God will give me a richer, deeper, more fulfilling life than ignoring it?

Church leaders and parents don't need to freak out when people ask these questions. In fact, they need to celebrate and patiently engage in discussions to answer them. If we're afraid of people asking them, we'll communicate that God's truth can't stand up to the strain of rigorous analysis. People don't grow without tests and tensions. The freedom to ask these questions (and many others) is the fertile soil of spiritual growth.

In my formative years, I asked a lot of questions. If I was going to base the rest of my life—and all of eternity—on the words in a book, I wanted to be thoroughly convinced it's reliable. In conversations with pastors and other church leaders, I asked, "How can a book with sixty-six parts by forty different authors and written over 1500 years be consistent? How do we know what we have today is what was originally written? How can something written during the Bronze Age be relevant in a society that put people on the moon?"

But that's not all. I also struggled with other questions that challenged my faith that were prompted by professors in college, friends, and articles in magazines, including:

- Don't all religions eventually lead people to God?

- Isn't the Bible filled with contradictions?

- Do people who don't believe in Jesus go to a literal hell where they're tormented for eternity?

- Is the way a person conducts his or her sex life really that important to God?

For a while, these questions consumed my thoughts and my conversations. Then, one day I read a passage in John's Gospel. "Jesus said to those Jews who believed in Him, 'If you abide in my word, you are my disciples indeed. And you shall know the truth and the truth shall make you free'" (John 8:31–32). Suddenly, I realized the proper order of things: If I believe and trust God, the Word of God will then make sense, and the truth will make me free. Belief comes before understanding; trust precedes illumination.

WHAT IS TRUTH?

One of the most important questions any of us can ask is, What is truth? Or to put it another way, How can we really know what we think we know? What can we actually count on? What's the foundation of facts and principles on which we can build our lives? When Jesus met Pilate, the governor wasn't sure what to make of the man standing in front of him. Jesus had been beaten to a pulp, yet He made the bold claim to be a king: "My kingdom is not of this world. If My kingdom were of this world, My servants would fight, so that I should not be delivered to the Jews; but now My kingdom is not from here."

Pilate was surprised. He blurted out, "Are You a king then?"

Jesus told him, "You say rightly that I am a king. For this cause I was born, and for this cause I have come into the world, that I should bear witness to the truth. Everyone who is of the truth hears My voice" (John 18:36–37).

When I read this passage, I had to ask myself, Am I on the side of truth? Do I listen to Jesus?

Listening means much more than hearing. It includes responding in obedience. Is that how I react to the truth Jesus spoke and still speaks? If not, then something else is my highest authority, my source of truth, and my God—it may be a philosophy, a religion, a person, a substance, a career, or a pursuit of any kind. Something will be my God. Will it be the real God or a counterfeit?

God's truth isn't optional. We can't grow without it. In Jesus' great prayer before His arrest, He asked the Father to do a work in us: "Sanctify them by Your truth. Your word is truth" (John 17:17). But God knows that the deception and temptation our first parents experienced in the Garden are still problems for us today. God has called pastors and teachers to explain the Word so disciples can know how to apply it. In the church, though, those who preach and teach will find some people eager to respond in faith as well as others who could care less about God's truth. Paul explained this fact to his protégé, Timothy:

Preach the word! Be ready in season and out of season. Convince, rebuke, exhort, with all longsuffering and teaching. For the time will come when they will not endure sound doctrine, but according to their own desires, because they have itching ears, they will heap up for themselves teachers; and they will turn their ears away from the truth, and be turned aside to fables. (2 Timothy 4:2–4)

I'm afraid that time is here. A lot of people go to church each week looking for pastors and teachers who will tell them what they want to hear. Disciples have already determined to hear and heed the Word, even if they don't like it, even when it's inconvenient, and even when it challenges their lifestyles. If the Word is truth, then anything that disagrees with it is a lie. Every time disciples read or hear God's truth, they have predetermined to trust it and obey it.

REASONS TO BELIEVE

As I wrestled with the questions of faith and truth, and as I chose to believe God and let Him convince me about the Bible, I came to several important conclusions.

1. Believing the Word of God is the only option that makes sense.

Atheism doesn't make sense because it says everything in the universe happened by chance, so there's no higher moral law or code of ethics to govern life. The survival of the fittest rules, and kindness is an obstacle to advancement.

New Age concepts don't make sense because they claim we're each evolving into gods. (I'm sure not, and I have serious doubts about you!) And besides that, the people who follow that teaching are a bit too odd for me.

Hinduism doesn't make sense because you have to believe there are countless gods and we're constantly being reincarnated to try to do better in the next life. If I live a good life, I may come back as a deer or a bear, but if not, I might be a mosquito.

Buddhism doesn't make sense because it's based on the teaching of a man who claimed to find a path to enlightenment apart from any input from God.

Islam doesn't make sense because it insists we trust a man who had slaves, concubines, twelve wives, and who founded a religion that—as practiced by some—rewards violence against anyone who disagrees with them.

Trusting in the authority of God's
Word gives us wisdom and security
in a changing world.

As I read the Bible, the truth about God, about people, and about life resonated with me. It tells me I'm a sinner, but that God made the ultimate sacrifice to take the punishment I deserve. It made sense that following Jesus is much more than drudgery; it's the greatest adventure life can offer. And it made sense that the unchangeable truths in God's Word apply today just as they applied to cultures thousands of years ago because human nature and human needs haven't changed.

Trusting in the authority of God's Word gives us wisdom and security in a changing world. At the end of His most famous message, Jesus told us:

> "Therefore whoever hears these sayings of Mine, and does them, I will liken him to a wise man who built his house on the rock: and the rain descended, the floods came, and the winds blew and beat on that house; and it did not fall, for it was founded on the rock. But everyone who hears these sayings of Mine, and does not do them, will be like a foolish man who built his house on the sand: and the rain descended, the floods came, and the winds blew and beat on that house; and it fell. And great was its fall." (Matthew 7:24–27)

Foolishness is willful blindness to the consequences of bad choices. Wise people anticipate the outcome of their decisions, and their choices add value to themselves and others. Fools don't care how their dumb decisions hurt others and mess up their own lives, and they deny any responsibility. Jesus is saying, "Don't be a fool. Make Me and My Word the foundation for your life. That's the way I've designed life to work."

2. The Bible has proven to be the most prophetically accurate book of all time.

Excellent and scholarly books have been written about the amazing accuracy of the prophesies in the Bible. They have identified more than 300 specific prophesies about the coming of the Messiah. Here are just a few:

- He would be born in Bethlehem (Micah 5:2).

- He would be born of a virgin (Isaiah 7:14).

- He would come from the tribe of Judah (Genesis 49:10).

- He would have to flee to Egypt (Hosea 11:1).

- He would be rejected by his own people (Isaiah 53:3).

- He would be the Son of God (Psalm 2:7).

- He would be crucified (Psalm 22:12–18).

- His hands and feet would be pierced (Psalm 22:16).

- He would be buried in a rich man's tomb (Isaiah 53:9).

- He would rise from the dead (Psalm 16:10).

- He would ascend to the right hand of God (Psalm 68:18).

Many unbelievers have tried to discount the authenticity of the Gospels, but as archeologists search ancient sites, they find even more evidence that the accounts are historically accurate. In *The Case for Christ*, former skeptic Lee Strobel quotes a scholar:

> "The general consensus of both liberal and conservative scholars is that Luke is very accurate as a historian. He's erudite, he's eloquent, his Greek approaches classical quality, he writes as an educated man, and archeological discoveries are showing over and over again that Luke is accurate in what he has to say."[4]

Strobel explains that in several instances, scholars who had been convinced Luke had a detail wrong in his Gospel or in Acts later made discoveries that confirmed Luke's account. We can trust the historical accuracy of the Bible.

3. Jesus always referred to the Word as the final authority.

We might question the validity of the Bible, but Jesus didn't. Some students of the Gospels claim that one tenth of Jesus' statements are either references to or direct quotations from Old Testament passages. When He was tempted by Satan in the wilderness, Jesus told him, "It is written, 'Man shall not live by bread alone, but by every word that proceeds from the mouth of God'" (Matthew 4:4). Later He taught, "Heaven and earth will pass away, but My words will by no means pass away" (Mark 13:31).

At the times of greatest distress in His life, in the Garden of Gethsemane and on the cross, Jesus was filled with the truth of the Word. It can be said that when you cut Jesus, He bled Scripture.

4. I've seen God's Word work powerfully in the lives of people.

These principles about the authority of God's truth aren't just academic and theoretical. I've witnessed the power of God's Word in my own life and the lives of countless others. I've seen hopeless people find a new reason to live as they read the pages of the Bible. I know people who were bound in the slavery of addictions to drugs, alcohol, sex, food, or gambling who found power to break free and find a life of love and meaning. I've seen broken marriages healed by the forgiveness the struggling couples found in the Word, and I've seen prodigals come to their senses and come home when God spoke to them through His truth. I've watched sick people be healed and demons cast out of those who were possessed as leaders and friends claimed the power of God through the Word.

> If we're free at all, hopeful at all, and effective at all, it's because God's Word is at work in and through us.

If we're free at all, hopeful at all, and effective at all, it's because God's Word is at work in and through us.

THE LENS

If you're going to make the shift from a believer to a disciple, you'll have to decide to use the Word of God as your lens for viewing every person, possession, and pursuit in your life. Other lenses must be identified and rejected. For most of us, this isn't an easy task because we have to make some important commitments:

1. We exalt the Word over our feelings.

Today, people live by their emotions. Decades ago, our shifting cultural standards declared, "If it feels good, do it." This philosophy is more alive today than ever. We want what we want, and we want it now!

God created us with emotions, so those emotions aren't wrong in themselves, but they must be submitted to God or they can certainly lead us in the wrong direction. When someone hurts us, our desire to hurt the person back can consume us if we disregard all those passages we read about forgiving others just as Christ has forgiven us! If we're climbing the corporate ladder to get promotions and advance our careers, do we feel justified in using people and shading the truth to take the next step up? When we're driving along and someone cuts us off, do we believe that person's disregard for our safety justifies our ugly outbursts? We can come up with a million reasons to live by our feelings. Many young people come to Christ when they're involved in a sexual relationship outside marriage. Those new believers feel torn between two competing desires: to follow Christ or to continue sinning in the relationship.

Believers continue to be controlled by their emotions, but disciples are controlled by the truth of Scripture. I'm not saying their powerful emotions will instantly change as they choose to obey God rather than their feelings. Anger, hurt, fear, and inordinate desires may linger, but disciples make choices based on truth, not feelings.

2. We move from only hearing the Word to obeying it.

Believers can hear messages and read passages of Scripture, but they wait to be moved, they wait to be convinced that it matters to them, and they wait until all their questions are answered. Disciples have a predisposition to act on what they hear and read. They don't come to church to be entertained. They come to be directed by God. They're already moving forward, eager to do whatever God tells them to do. They certainly ask plenty of questions, but their questions aren't meant to delay or distract. Their questions are designed to bring clarity and wisdom so they can act more assertively.

James, the half-brother of Jesus, was a man of action. He said it's easy to hear and forget, but a disciple hears and obeys. He wrote, "Be doers of the word, and not hearers only, deceiving yourselves. For if anyone is a hearer of the word and not a doer, he is like a man observing his natural face in a mirror; for he observes himself, goes away, and immediately forgets what kind of man he was. But he who looks into the perfect law of liberty and continues in it, and is not a forgetful hearer but a doer of the work, this one will be blessed in what he does" (James 1:22–25).

Do you want God to pour out His blessings on you? Be a doer of the Word.

3. We believe God's Word never fails, regardless of the circumstances.

At different points and in different ways, God tests us to see if we'll trust Him or if we'll give up. This shouldn't be a surprise to anyone who reads the Bible. The list of heroes in Hebrews 11 doesn't include people who had it easy. They were men and women who faced extreme stress and heartache. They were heroes because they refused to give up or give in. They kept trusting God in the dark, in the storm, and in the silence. Sometimes God miraculously rescued them or used them to rescue others, but sometimes He didn't. Even then, those people trusted that God would be fully faithful, truly trustworthy in the next life.

God's promises are sure, though it may seem God is very slow to answer them. In a beautiful description of His promise, God spoke through Isaiah:

"'For My thoughts are not your thoughts,
　Nor are your ways My ways,' says the Lord.
　'For as the heavens are higher than the earth,
　So are My ways higher than your ways,
　And My thoughts than your thoughts.

For as the rain comes down, and the snow from heaven,
And do not return there,
But water the earth,
And make it bring forth and bud,
That it may give seed to the sower
And bread to the eater,
So shall My word be that goes forth from My mouth;
It shall not return to Me void,
But it shall accomplish what I please,
And it shall prosper in the thing for which I sent it.'"
(Isaiah 55:8–11)

The law of sowing and reaping means we reap *what* we sow, we reap *after* we sow, and we reap *more than* we sow. When we understand this concept, we can wait for the answer with at least a little more faith and patience.

When we're tested, we cry out to the Lord in our anguish. Half of the Psalms are laments in which the writer pours out a heart of disappointment, sorrow, confusion, and anger. But sooner or later, God gives the writer a new perspective, a new lens with which to look at the situation, and a new sense of hope that God will eventually accomplish His purposes. In the same way, God invites us to pour out our hearts to Him. As we're honest with God about the tests we face, we open our eyes to see Him more clearly, and we open our hearts to trust Him more fully.

We can count on the promises of God, even if they aren't fulfilled in our timeframe. The law of sowing and reaping means we reap *what* we sow, we reap *after* we sow, and we reap *more than* we sow. When we understand this concept, we can wait for the answer with at least a little more faith and patience.

When I sold my business and moved to Richmond, I expected to find a job very quickly. After months of looking, however, I hadn't found anything, and my financial resources were drying up. I had never been at this place before: I would soon have no money, but I still had bills to pay. I had been tithing and serving, but the door to every job opportunity remained closed. I felt confused and desperate. One day I came to the startling conclusion that if something didn't happen really soon, I wouldn't be able to pay the rent on my apartment, and I'd be homeless. This wasn't exactly the abundant life I expected when I decided to follow Jesus!

One Sunday afternoon I prayed, "God, either Your Word is true and You provide for Your people, or it's not true and I need to move on with my life without You. Either way, I need to know what's true, and I need to know really fast!" I could have called my dad and asked for some money, but I didn't want to do that. I said, "God, I'm willing to be homeless and lose my car, but I'm going to trust You and Your Word."

I had scheduled some interviews for the next day, but I sensed God telling me to cancel those meetings. Instead, He directed me to go back to a company where I'd already applied for jobs three times.

The next morning, I drove over to the company and walked into the corporate office. I told the receptionist, "I'd like to see Mr. Hunt."

"Is he expecting you?" she asked.

"No, but I think he'll see me."

"I'm sorry," she explained, "but he's in a meeting all morning. I'll be glad to let him know you came by when he comes out of his meeting."

Very calmly I asked, "Would you please tell him Dennis Rouse is here to see him?"

She looked puzzled at the combination of my insistence and my pleasant demeanor. She said, "Well, okay." She got up and opened the door to a room near her. I could see through the window as she approached a man and whispered something to him. A few seconds later, she came back, looking somewhat startled. "Mr. Hunt said he wants to talk to you. Please go into his office and have a seat. He'll be with you as soon as he finishes his meeting."

She showed me to Mr. Hunt's office where I sat for about thirty minutes. When he walked in, he smiled and asked, "Dennis, what brings you here?"

I said, "I'm applying for the job opening. I think I can do a good job for you and the company."

Mr. Hunt looked at my application and then leaned back in his chair. He said, "It looks like you have the experience we're looking for, and you have the qualifications, but there's a problem on your application."

I'm sure I looked surprised. He continued, "Under hobbies, you put 'serving God.' We don't like people to be hyper-religious, and besides, when people are too much into their faith, most of them don't stay around very long. They're always looking for something else, like becoming a pastor. This causes some concerns for me. We're looking for somebody who will fit in well with our company and be committed to the job."

I told him honestly, "Sir, going into the ministry is the last thing on my mind. I think I can do a good job for you, and I'll fit in here."

He asked, "When can you start?"

I was ready to start that minute, but we agreed for me to come back the next morning. I went home rejoicing. By that time, Colleen and I had started dating, so I called to tell her the good news. After we celebrated for a few minutes, she asked, "When do you get your first check?"

I hadn't thought about that. I gulped and said, "In two weeks." Instantly, both of us knew I had to pay my rent that Friday or I'd be out on the street. At that moment, the Lord said, "Go look at today's mail."

When I opened the mailbox, I saw a letter from my grandparents in Florida. They seldom wrote me, so I was interested to see what they'd said. My grandmother wrote, "We were thinking about you, and we wanted to send you some money." They had sent a check for $500! It covered all my bills and left a few dollars for groceries for the next couple of weeks.

My heart was about to explode. Only the day before, I wondered if God's Word would fail and I'd be spiritually and literally homeless, but God orchestrated two supernatural events to provide in a way that demonstrated His power, His love, and maybe a bit of His humor. I could sure imagine God smiling during all that!

From that day to this, I've never doubted God would provide for me financially. He hasn't always provided the way I expected or in the time I hoped He would, but I've always had confidence He would come through . . . and He has.

I don't want to live a normal life. I want to live the abundant life, an adventure hand-in-hand with Jesus, a purpose-driven life. I want my life to count, to have an impact on the people around me. None of this can happen apart from the Word of God illuminating the greatness and grace of Jesus, transforming my motives and desires so I want God's best more than anything else in the world, and empowering me to live wholeheartedly for God and His kingdom.

> I don't want to live a normal life. I want to live the abundant life, an adventure hand-in-hand with Jesus, a purpose-driven life.

Does the truth of the Bible bore you or thrill you? The writer to the Hebrews tells us, "The word of God is living and powerful, and sharper than any two-edged sword, piercing even to the division of soul and spirit, and of joints and marrow, and is a discerner of the thoughts and intents of the heart" (Hebrews 4:12). If you are open to it, the Word of God will perform surgery, heal your heart, and give you more power than you ever thought possible.

Invite God to use His Word to do powerful things in your soul.

THINK ABOUT IT:

1. Why is it necessary to wrestle with hard questions about God's Word? What happens when we either aren't allowed or aren't willing to ask them?

2. What are some threats to the truth of God in our culture today? How does our trust in the authority of the Word give us security and confidence to obey God?

3. Why do feelings seem to be the ultimate authority in our lives? What happens to our faith and our relationships when we live by our feelings instead of God's truth?

4. What are some ways you can tell if you're a doer of the Word and not just a hearer?

5. What are some severe tests faced by people you know? Which people have trusted God and His Word through those tests? What happened to them as a result?

6. What are some practical ways you can read and study the Bible so it penetrates your heart and transforms every aspect of your life?

7. On a scale of 0 (nada) to 10 (the ultimate), rate yourself as a disciple who loves the Word, studies the Word, and obeys the Word. Explain your answer. How might you improve your rating?

CHAPTER 6

A DISCIPLE . . .
LIVES MORALLY PURE

ll people are born with a powerful inward bent: we love to sin. The word often conjures up acts like rape, murder, and stealing, but also includes all the "self sins": selfishness, self-justification, self-righteousness, and self-pity. No matter how much we're told sin is harmful and will mess up our lives, those attitudes and actions seem reasonable and desirable. In fact, they appear to be absolutely necessary for our happiness. That's the nature of temptation, one of Satan's most powerful weapons. He tries to make us believe sin is the only rational path to a meaningful life. Without it, we're nothing.

I'm not talking about something that's foreign to me. After I trusted in Jesus, the biggest challenge of my spiritual life was the issue of sin vs. purity. Sin didn't have to sneak up on me. I embraced it! I loved to sin. It was my greatest joy and my constant pursuit. When I thought about the changes God wanted to make in my life, I immediately concluded, "I can't do that! There's no way I can give up sex and partying and all that comes with them. That's what I enjoy most in life!"

God had to do some deep work in my mind and my heart to change my perspective. It's my guess—no, it's my conviction—that God has already done or wants to do some deep work in your life, too. We need God to open our eyes to alert us to the seriousness and destructiveness of sin, and we also need Him to give us a deeper experience of His forgiveness and purpose than ever before.

SLAVERY AND FREEDOM

Human bondage has been a reality since history began. Conquered people often became slaves of their enemies. In the seventeenth and eighteenth centuries, Europeans kidnapped and enslaved millions of Africans and sent them to the New World to work on plantations. This type of slavery is part of our history and perhaps most familiar to us, but there are other forms. In the Roman world, people who owed large debts could become indentured servants for a few years. When those debts were paid by their service, the people became free again. Quite often, those "slaves" were more educated than their masters. A very different kind of slavery exists in today's world. Some authorities estimate that when we include sex slaves and people trapped in dependence on grueling manual labor, there are almost 46 million slaves today.[5]

The Bible says all people are slaves to sin, in the grips of a cruel master with no hope of securing freedom on our own. The price of freedom requires a costly payment, the redemption paid by a perfect person. Only because of Christ, we've been set free!

In his letter to the Colossians, Paul used two terms to describe our condition before Jesus set us free: we were dead and we were slaves of Satan—not a hopeful combination! He wrote: "You were dead because of your sins and because your sinful nature was not yet cut away. Then God made you alive with Christ, for he forgave all our sins. He canceled the record of the charges against us and took it away by nailing it to the cross. In this way, he disarmed the spiritual rulers and authorities. He shamed them publicly by his victory over them on the cross" (Colossians 2:13–15, NLT).

When people couldn't pay their bills in the Roman world, they were thrown in debtor's prison and a list of their unpaid bills was nailed to the cell door. Paul says that our list of debts—every sin we've ever committed and ever will commit—was taken from our cell door and nailed to Jesus' cell door, the cross, where He stayed until they were paid. John records that the last words of Jesus on the cross were "It is finished," which means "Paid in full" (John 19:30).

The fact that our sins are forgiven and we've received the presence and power of the Holy Spirit is the undeniable, incontrovertible truth of the Christian faith. The problem is that there's another fact: the enemy of our souls wants us to doubt this truth and continue to live, at least to some degree, in slavery.

Is it even possible that someone who has been set free at enormous cost still chooses to live in slavery? Yes, it has happened. The American Civil War was fought primarily over the issue of slavery. About 700,000 men died in that horrible conflict. When it was over, the Constitution was amended to ensure all the Southern slaves were forever free. The papers were signed and laws were decreed, but many of the slaves who had lived their entire lives on plantations chose to stay and work for the people who had owned them. Many former slaves became sharecroppers, living much as they had lived as property. Rivers of blood had been spilled to set them free, but they continued to live in a condition much like bondage.

> The fact that our sins are forgiven and we've received the presence and power of the Holy Spirit is the undeniable, incontrovertible truth of the Christian faith.

Countless Christians today do the same. They have been set free by blood shed for them, but they still live under sin's domination. Satan, sin's slave master, whispers, "You're not really free. You can't make it on your own. Look what you'll have to give up if you really live in freedom. You're safer with me."

How do we avoid voluntarily returning to slavery after Jesus sets us free? In one of the most important parts of Paul's letter to the Christians in Rome, he explains that we identify with Jesus in His death and His resurrection. In those truths, we find an answer to sin's hold on us. When Jesus died on the cross, we were "in Him." That means all the power of His forgiveness is unleashed on our sins. And when Jesus came out of the tomb, we were "in Him," and He gives us a new life. Paul explained it this way: "Knowing this, that our old man was crucified with Him, that the body of sin might be done away with, that we should no longer be slaves of sin. For he who has died has been freed from sin. Now if we died with Christ, we believe that we shall also live with Him" (Romans 6:6–8).

When sin is hard to shake and doubt clouds our minds, Paul tells us to think! Consider, ponder, analyze, and believe that the death and resurrection of Jesus applies to us today, right now, in this moment! He wrote, "For the death that He died, He died to sin once for all; but the life that He lives, He lives to God. Likewise you also, reckon yourselves to be dead indeed to sin, but alive to God in Christ Jesus our Lord" (Romans 6:10–11).

This magnificent truth is more than academic theology we find in a book. It's the way we experience freedom, power, and joy every minute of every day. When we're tempted, we look back to Jesus and realize His way is best. When we're ashamed, we look back to Jesus and thank Him for His full payment for our sins. When we feel hopeless, we look back at Jesus and remember that He conquered death by coming out of the grave.

Paul said the answer is a very practical one—we choose life over death and freedom over bondage: "Therefore do not let sin reign in your mortal body, that you should obey it in its lusts. And do not present your members as instruments of unrighteousness to sin, but present yourselves to God as being alive from the dead, and your members as instruments of righteousness to God. For sin shall not have dominion over you, for you are not under law but under grace" (Romans 6:12–14). We face these choices all day, every day.

GOOD COMPANY

It sounds clear and simple, doesn't it? Wouldn't anybody choose freedom over slavery? You'd think so, but why, then, is so much of the Bible a warning about the dangers of sin and instructions about how to live holy lives? It's because sin is so seductive and powerful.

If you have difficulty living in the freedom of grace and the power of the Spirit, you're not alone. Every hero of the Bible wrestled with sin. We think of Abraham as the father of our faith, but he lied (twice) to save his skin when powerful rulers inquired about his beautiful wife. Abraham said she was only his sister (which was a half-truth). David was a brilliant leader and a brave soldier, but he committed adultery and then murdered the woman's husband to keep him from finding out she was pregnant. Solomon was the richest and most powerful king in Israel's history, but he had a thing about women that eventually undermined all his incredible wisdom. Peter proclaimed he would never betray Jesus . . . just hours before he denied (to a servant girl) that he even knew Him. Paul was involved with the capture, imprisonment, and execution of multitudes of Christians before Jesus met him on the Road to Damascus. Even though he became one of the greatest leaders the world has ever known, he described himself in one of his last letters as "the chief of sinners" (1 Timothy 1:15).

We get a window on Paul's struggle against sin in the very next chapter of his letter to the Romans. As he begins to describe the tension between good and evil in his own life, he first defends God's laws and commandments: They point out sin, but they don't cause sin. He then continues:

"So the trouble is not with the law, for it is spiritual and good. The trouble is with me, for I am all too human, a slave to sin. I don't really understand myself, for I want to do what is right, but I don't do it. Instead, I do what I hate. But if I know that what I am doing is wrong, this shows that I agree that the law is good. So I am not the one doing wrong; it is sin living in me that does it" (Romans 7:14–17, NLT).

His was no quick confession. Paul goes into detail to articulate what was going on in his mind and heart: "I know that nothing good lives in me, that is, in my sinful nature. I want to do what is right, but I can't. I want to

If you're at all interested in following Jesus and being a true disciple, you experience the conflict Paul is talking about.

do what is good, but I don't. I don't want to do what is wrong, but I do it anyway. But if I do what I don't want to do, I am not really the one doing wrong; it is sin living in me that does it. I have discovered this principle of life—that when I want to do what is right, I inevitably do what is wrong" (Romans 7:18–21, NLT).

Have you discovered this principle too? Of course, you have. If you're at all interested in following Jesus and being a true disciple, you experience the conflict Paul is talking about. You and I sometimes want to shout, with Paul, "I love God's law with all my heart. But there is another power within me that is at war with my mind. This power makes me a slave to the sin that is still within me. Oh, what a miserable person I am! Who will free me from this life that is dominated by sin and death?" (Romans 7:22–24, NLT)

Is there an answer? Yes, it's the one Paul has unfolded in the first six chapters of this remarkable letter, and he repeats it here: "Thank God! The answer is in Jesus Christ our Lord. So you see how it is: In my mind I really want to obey God's law, but because of my sinful nature I am a slave to sin. So now there is no condemnation for those who belong to Christ Jesus" (Romans 7:25–8:1, NLT).

If the man who met Jesus and became the leader of the church in the first century admits his struggle with sin, you and I can admit our struggles, too. It's a fight, it's a war, and no one is exempt from active duty. The question is: Will we fight well?

THE FIGHT

For disciples to fight with wisdom and strength, we need to understand how sin works in our minds and hearts. We can identify four aspects of sin . . . we might identify them as stages, but all the parts soon become ingrained and integrated.

The lure

At first, sin is attractive. It calls out to us that it will fulfill our deepest longings. It offers wonderful promises, and we believe them. Sin isn't limited to crimes punishable by law; it's putting anyone or anything in the place of God in our lives. It's making God secondary and something else primary. There's nothing wrong with beauty, pleasure, excitement, power, and approval if those things are gifts from the hand of God and we hold them lightly. But even very good things can become sinful pursuits if we want them more than we want God.

Paul sometimes includes lists of sins that are representative, but of course, aren't exhaustive. In his first letter to the Corinthians, he wrote, "Don't you realize that those who do wrong will not inherit the Kingdom of God? Don't fool yourselves. Those who indulge in sexual sin, or who worship idols, or commit adultery, or are male prostitutes, or practice homosexuality, or are thieves, or greedy people, or drunkards, or are abusive, or cheat people—none of these will inherit the Kingdom of God. Some of you were once like that. But you were cleansed; you were made holy; you were made right with God by calling on the name of the Lord Jesus Christ and by the Spirit of our God" (1 Corinthians 6:9–11, NLT).

And in Paul's last letter, one to Timothy, his son in the faith, he warned: "You should know this, Timothy, that in the last days there will be very difficult times. For people will love only themselves and their money. They will be boastful and proud, scoffing at God, disobedient to their parents, and ungrateful. They will consider nothing sacred. They will be unloving and unforgiving; they will slander others and have no self-control. They will be cruel and hate what is good. They will betray their friends, be reckless, be puffed up with pride, and love pleasure rather than God. They will act religious, but they will reject the power that could make them godly. Stay away from people like that!" (2 Timothy 3:1–5, NLT)

We might want to wag our fingers at some of "those people" who sin so blatantly, but sin isn't only about the worst things people do. It's also about attitudes and motives: loving ourselves more than God, being ungrateful for all God has given to us, holding grudges instead of pouring out the forgiveness Jesus has poured into us, loving pleasure, and acting religious to impress people. Do any of those labels fit you? Undoubtedly.

The drive

We not only believe the promises of our culture; we're driven by them to long for more and more. God has made us so that only He can fill the gaping hole in our souls. When we try to fill it with people, power, pleasure, or possessions, we get a quick hit of satisfaction, but soon we feel just as empty again. Our solution is to double-down and go for more of the things that can't satisfy. When that leaves us empty, we may be confused, but we try even harder.

Our incessant drive to sin becomes a spiritual stronghold, a fortress of belief and desire that is fortified by the enemy's lies, our culture's promises, and our own foolishness to believe those things. It's not hard to recognize addictions to alcohol and drugs, but sin has a more elusive, though just as addictive, quality. Addicts experience "tolerance": after a while, the effect of the substance diminishes, so they require more of it, or a more powerful substance, to achieve the same high. In the same way, our thirst for approval, entertainment, power over others, or control of life's circumstances is insatiable—no matter how much we get, it's never enough. We always crave more.

We're exposed to the lure and the drive of sin all day, every day. Every billboard, television commercial, and magazine ad has two promises: one on the surface and one underneath. The surface promise is that the toothpaste will clean your teeth and the Internet provider will give you good service. If we look closely, however, we recognize the hidden promise is that the toothpaste will give you the friends you've always wanted and the Internet provider will make your life incredibly pleasant and meaningful. The hidden promises are the ones that capture our hearts and lure us into the trap. When we believe we deserve a hassle-free life, complete joy, and the absence of conflict, we're devastated by the reality of the real world when it inevitably crashes our party.

> We're exposed to the lure and the drive of sin all day, every day. Every billboard, television commercial, and magazine ad has two promises: one on the surface and one underneath.

In many ways, we're products of the messages that surround us. Marketing matters: we're repeatedly exposed to a constant stream of ads that tell us we can't be secure, loved, or happy without a particular product or service . . . and we believe them. In *The Technological Society,* Jacque Ellul noted that advertising is designed to create an expectation—a demand—for an ideal life of ease, plenty, and fun. He asserts that this misplaced expectation consumes our desires and seriously erodes our spiritual values.[6] Similarly, in an article posted on CNN's website, Monita Rajpal observed,

> Everywhere we go, everywhere we look, we are inundated with messages. We don't even have to think for ourselves. All we have to do is sit on our comfy couch and be told how to live our lives. From how to look, what to wear, what to eat, what our homes should look like, how to meet people, what to drive, practically every facet of our lives is taken care of. That is the power of advertising. . . . In this age of multiple mediums, advertising is everywhere—whether it's a pop-up campaign with people dancing at the train station (T-Mobile) that serves a multitude of platforms from television to the web, or a home-video-type commercial that is posted on YouTube. We may not have to think for ourselves as much but we do have to be more discriminating to decipher what is credible and what isn't. Bottom line though, advertising is a part of our existence. The good news is we're the ones with the power to choose.[7]

How can we assess the impact of advertising on our lives? If we review our thoughts for a day, what will we notice? How much do we think about buying an item or subscribing to a service that will make us more attractive, win the approval of our friends, make us more successful, or impress people around us? And how much do we worry about losing those things? The impact of advertising is incredibly strong . . . and incredibly insidious.

The lifestyle

I've talked to alcoholics who have told me, "Dennis, everything in my life revolved around drinking. I thought about getting a bottle when I woke up in the morning, all day long at work, and on the way home. When I finally walked into the liquor store, I was achieving my secondary goal for the entire day. Of course, my first goal was to get drunk so I could forget about all the chaos with my family and at work—chaos I'd created by my drinking."

This preoccupation with a substance or behavior isn't just about whisky or prescription pills or pornography. Our lives revolve around whatever is the most important thing to us, and we can't stop thinking about it. Whenever we have a free moment, our minds dart back to ways we can have more of what we delight in, even if that thing, person, or pursuit is ruining our lives. We organize our time to get it, we use our money to have it, and we neglect other responsibilities to acquire it.

The "it" may be something others applaud (job promotions, fame as a leader, etc.), something that sets us apart from others (a boat, a fit body, fine jewelry, a big bank account), or something destructive like the addictions we often identify.

Building a lifestyle around such things is a natural result of responding to the wrong lures that created our self-destructive drives. For many people, the message of commercials and ads validates their self-absorbed lifestyles. Sooner or later, living for ourselves causes harm to us and those we love. When that happens, we try to find a way to cope with all the chaos.

The reactions

We're very creative people. We find all kinds of ways to cope with the mess we create by our lifestyles of sin. Some of us give up and give in.

We can't take it anymore, so we let others tell us what to do. We no longer have goals and plans; all those have died with our colossal failures. Others find ways to numb the pain, usually through various substances or mindless entertainment. Still others go in quite a different direction. The collapse of their dreams enflames anger, and they attack anyone who dares to speak the truth to them or hold them accountable. And of course, some of us are so gifted that we use two or three of these coping skills!

ALIKE BUT SO VERY DIFFERENT

When we notice the damage caused by our sin, we may respond with guilt or shame. These two reactions may look alike in some ways, but they have very different results. Guilt is feeling bad about something you did. It's God's wakeup call to confess sin, repent, and come back to Him. But shame is much deeper and darker; it's the conclusion that you not only *did* something bad, you *are* something bad. Guilt can lead to a wonderful restoration of our intimacy with God and the experience of joy and power. But shame crushes the spirit. We try to feel bad enough long enough to pay for what we've done. Instead of experiencing the joy of forgiveness, we try to prove we're good people who deserve God's acceptance. It doesn't work. It never has and it never will. In shame, we beat ourselves up, we call ourselves nasty names, and we try to feel so awful that God surely will think we're good people. After all, only really good people would feel that bad about messing up!

> Guilt can lead to a wonderful restoration of our intimacy with God and the experience of joy and power. But shame crushes the spirit.

To get relief from the soul-destroying impact of shame, we may return to sin so we can get a temporary high. Some sins release endorphins which give us pleasure for a while, but when we come down, the shame is even worse. Despising ourselves becomes a noose that tightens around our necks until it strangles the life out of us.

Paul acknowledges both these ways of responding to sin. His first letter to the Corinthian church included a scathing message to acknowledge some specific sins and to repent. It took a while before he heard from them, but after he did, his letter of 2 Corinthians praised them for responding in humility and faith. He draws a stark contrast between "godly sorrow," which is conviction and repentance, and "worldly sorrow," which is shame. He wrote, "Even if I caused you sorrow by my letter, I do not regret it. Though I did regret it—I see that my letter hurt you, but only for a little while—yet now I am happy, not because you were made sorry, but because your sorrow led you to repentance. For you became sorrowful as God intended and so were not harmed in any way by us. Godly sorrow brings repentance that leads to salvation and leaves no regret, but worldly sorrow brings death" (2 Corinthians 7:8–10, NIV).

Think of the younger brother in Jesus' story of the Prodigal Son. This son offended his father by demanding his share of the inheritance, and he wasted it all in a foreign land on wine, women, and song. His life was a disaster. As a young Jewish man, he found himself feeding pigs and longing to eat their slop. Then, he "came to his senses" and started his journey home. He carefully rehearsed his speech to his father to confess his sin and ask to become a hired hand on the farm. When his father saw him in the distance, he ran to his son, interrupted his confession, kissed him, and restored him to the family. This is an example of "godly sorrow" that brings repentance that "leads to salvation and leaves no regret." It's the kind of sorrow God wants us to experience after we sin, and it leads to a deeper appreciation of grace, a higher love for the God who forgives and restores, and a stronger desire to avoid being foolish again!

CONFESSION

Throughout church history, God's people have made a regular practice of confessing sin and being reminded of God's wonderful forgiveness. Today, I'm afraid we don't give enough weight to this important element of worship and discipleship. Confess means "to agree with." When we confess our sins, we agree with God that what we did was wrong, that our sins have already been forgiven by Jesus' payment on the cross, and that we need to make some practical changes.

In John's first letter, he reminds us that Jesus is "the light of the world," the one from whom darkness flees. Disciples are committed to live in the light of God's truth and grace—no matter what that light reveals in our hearts, our relationships, and our choices. It shouldn't surprise us when the Spirit of God shows us we've sinned. There's no need to be defensive or blame someone else. A disciple says, "Lord, you're right. That was wrong."

John explained that living in the light necessarily means we become skilled and quick to confess our sins:

This is the message which we have heard from Him and declare to you, that God is light and in Him is no darkness at all. If we say that we have fellowship with Him, and walk in darkness, we lie and do not practice the truth. But if we walk in the light as He is in the light, we have fellowship with one another, and the blood of Jesus Christ His Son cleanses us from all sin.

If we say that we have no sin, we deceive ourselves, and the truth is not in us. If we confess our sins, He is faithful and just to forgive us our sins and to cleanse us from all unrighteousness. If we say that we have not sinned, we make Him a liar, and His word is not in us. (1 John 1:5–10)

Confession, then, isn't something to avoid like the plague! It's God's supernatural plan for us to experience His forgiveness and return to His light. When the Spirit taps us on the shoulder and points out sin, we're foolish to say, "Not me!" Instead, we can pray, "Thank You for showing this to me. And thank You even more for forgiving me. Give me wisdom and strength to walk with You and honor You."

If you're going to move from being a believer to being a disciple, you have to let God shine His light in the dark parts of your heart. Satan and his angels are chained in darkness, but God and His people love the light. The demons have no power in the light. They operate only in the darkness of sin, accusation, deception, and confusion. Make no mistake: we're in a fierce spiritual battle. Satan and his demons love to use shame and denial to keep God's people away from God's power and love. We can anticipate the last battle here and now. In Revelation, John records the triumphant words of a voice from heaven:

"Now salvation, and strength, and the kingdom of our God, and the power of His Christ have come, for the accuser of our brethren, who accused them before our God day and night, has been cast down. And they overcame him by the blood of the Lamb and by the word of their testimony, and they did not love their lives to the death. Therefore rejoice, O heavens, and you who dwell in them! Woe to the inhabitants of the earth and the sea! For the devil has come down to you, having great wrath, because he knows that he has a short time." (Revelation 12:10–12)

Disciples trust in the blood of Jesus to forgive them when they confess their sin. They speak the glorious words of their testimony of His love and power. They make choices each moment of the day to live for Him instead of their own pleasure, power, and prestige.

FIND A FRIEND

We live in a fiercely individualistic society. Every product and program is evaluated on how it benefits the individual. When we read the Bible, however, we get a very different picture of the way God wants His kingdom to work. Certainly, every believer has the personal experience of repentance and redemption, but when we believe, we're adopted into the family of God. We belong to one another, we're a body with many parts, and we simply can't function properly as isolated Christians. Believers may conclude they can get enough of God on their own, but disciples know better. They know they can only thrive when they experience vital connections with other disciples.

Men, you need at least one other man who is a devoted disciple of Christ to encourage you and hold you accountable, and preferably, a small group of these men. And women, you need at least one woman and maybe a small group. The vulnerability and intimacy required for these "life on life" conversations necessitate same-gender discipleship relationships.

The importance of strong relationships shouldn't be a surprise to anyone who reads the New Testament. All but one of Paul's letters were written to churches or to pastors of churches. (Philemon was written to reconcile a man with his runaway slave, both of whom were Christians.) In verse after verse and chapter after chapter, Paul tells us to love one another as Jesus loves us, accept one another as Jesus accepts us, and forgive one another as Jesus forgives us. We belong to God, but we also belong to one another. King Solomon understood that wise people have strong, "iron sharpening iron" relationships (Proverbs 27:17). The Proverbs contain many clear instructions and warnings about the need for accountability. We'll look at only three of them:

- Where there is no counsel, the people fall;
  But in the multitude of counselors there is safety (Proverbs 11:14).

- A man who isolates himself seeks his own desire;
  He rages against all wise judgment (Proverbs 18:1).

- The way of a fool is right in his own eyes,
  But he who heeds counsel is wise (Proverbs 12:15).

What's Solomon's message to us? Don't be a fool! Don't think you can be a Lone Ranger and walk with God. We need people who speak the truth to us, especially when we don't want to hear it. Sin makes us want to hide or blame others instead of humbly repenting, but when we're drifting (or running) away from God, we need to listen to the voice of the Spirit through the lips of those who know us and love us enough to step into our mess and show us the way back. Left to ourselves, we think we see things clearly and that we're making good decisions. We need people to hold up a mirror to show us the truth.

> Left to ourselves, we think we see things clearly and that we're making good decisions. We need people to hold up a mirror to show us the truth.

Do you have someone like this? If you don't, you're only a believer . . . or maybe you're becoming a disciple and are determined to keep looking until you find someone. But let me give you a warning: Be very selective as you seek out this person. If you pick someone who is always nice and agreeable, you might enjoy coffee together, but you won't be pushed to live wholeheartedly for God. And if you choose someone who smothers you with attention and directions, you won't have the freedom to make your own decisions and grow. Don't be surprised if one person doesn't work out and you need to find someone else. Just don't quit. Find someone who will push you and pull you into a deeper walk with God and radical obedience to Him. And soon, you'll become that kind of friend to others. It works that way.

PROTECT YOUR HEART

I can almost hear Paul sitting with people he discipled and telling them, "Hey, don't be stupid. If you have a pattern of sin, change the pattern. If you find yourself thinking about sinning in some way—sex or money or power or anything else—fix your mind on God and His purposes. And if you have magazines, books, websites, or apps [Okay, Paul didn't have those things, but stay with me here!] that draw your heart away from God, do whatever it takes to shut those out and shut them off!"

We're not helpless and powerless against sin. God has given us the truth of His Word, the power of the Spirit, the encouragement of others, and the will to make choices. Most of us don't have dozens of things that trip us up; we generally have only a few, and maybe only one or two. If we know that a certain magazine inflames our desire to have more stuff so we can't stop thinking about our next purchase, we need to cancel the subscription and throw away the old copies. If we've been frequenting websites that inflame inordinate passions, we need to buy software that blocks those sites. If we know that particular people or places tend to cause us to drift away from God, we need to avoid those places and either avoid those people or grow stronger so we can live for Christ as we interact with them. And if we become consumed with thoughts that don't honor God, we need to rivet our minds on the things above.

Sin starts in the mind, and purity starts there, too. We can't stop every evil, impure thought from running through our heads, but we can choose whether they take root or not. Paul knew the real fight happens between our ears, and it's nothing short of spiritual warfare. He wrote, "For though we walk in the flesh, we do not war according to the flesh.

For the weapons of our warfare are not carnal but mighty in God for pulling down strongholds, casting down arguments and every high thing that exalts itself against the knowledge of God, bringing every thought into captivity to the obedience of Christ" (2 Corinthians 10:3–5).

The messages in our culture promise love, fulfillment, and pleasure as a result of running away from God and indulging our desires. Believers try to walk the line between righteousness and sin, but disciples realize sin poisons their hearts and limits their effectiveness. But let's be honest: we still sin, we still drift, and we still make dumb choices. Moral purity, then, involves two choices: first to make good decisions to honor God with every fiber of our being, and then whenever we fail, to confess, repent, and reorient our lives around the pardon, presence, and purposes of God. Both commitments are essential.

Why would we want to be morally pure? Is it only to prove to people that we're good Christians, a moralistic notch on our belts? I'm afraid there are a lot of people with that motivation, but it only produces arrogance when we're doing better than someone else and self-pity when we're not. That's not the life of the Spirit! In John's first letter, he explains why we should want to be pure: "See what great love the Father has lavished on us, that we should be called children of God! And that is what we are! The reason the world does not know us is that it did not know him. Dear friends, now we are children of God, and what we will be has not yet been made known. But we know that when Christ appears, we shall be like him, for we shall see him as he is. All who have this hope in him purify themselves, just as he is pure" (1 John 3:1–3, NIV).

A disciple's pursuit of purity isn't a self-improvement program, and it isn't to impress other people. Disciples are overwhelmed by the wonder of the gospel of grace: we're forgiven, loved, and adopted by the King of glory! When Christ appears, all tears will be wiped away and all sin obliterated from the earth. The present reality of God's love and our ultimate hope of being with Him face to face is all the motivation we need to make choices to honor Him consistently.

We protect our hearts in many different ways, and all of them are important. We ruthlessly eliminate distractions and temptations; we focus our thoughts on God's love and His purposes; and we continually feed our souls with the wonder that He considers us His greatest treasure. Being a disciple is a delight and a fight. God has given us Christ's righteousness (2 Corinthians 5:21; Philippians 3:8–9), so we stand on solid ground. All we've received from God are gifts of His grace. In spite of our sins and failures, Jesus loves us, paid the ultimate price for our salvation, and gives us His Spirit to empower us to live for Him. Jesus died for us, and we choose to die for Him by giving up selfish desires so we can pursue Him and His kingdom with all our hearts. God has given us freedom, but not to be self-indulgent. We've been set free so we can devote ourselves to Him and His cause.

Has God spoken to you through the message of this chapter? Listen to Him and act on whatever He has told you.

THINK ABOUT IT:

1. Identify three or four memorable and recent television commercials or magazine ads. In each one, what's "the promise under the promise"? What do those hidden promises tell us about human nature (and ourselves)?

2. What are some ways sin makes us slaves? Does it encourage you or discourage you that Paul wrestled with sin (which he described in Romans 7)? Explain your answer.

3. What are some differences between "godly sorrow" and "worldly sorrow"? What are the results of both? Which of these have you experienced most often? How did it affect your heart, your relationship with God, and your other relationships?

4. What part should confession play in the life of a disciple? Do you really desire to live in the light? Why or why not?

5. What are some very practical ways you can protect your heart?

6. What is a disciple's motive for moral purity? How is it different from a believer's motive?

7. On a scale of 0 (not in the least) to 10 (all day, every day), how much are you committed to honor Christ with a pure life? Explain your answer. What needs to change in your life?

CHAPTER 7

A DISCIPLE IS . . . EVANGELISTICALLY BOLD

Did the last chapter on moral purity make you feel uncomfortable? I hope so, but we're just getting started! Another characteristic of a disciple of Jesus is being evangelistically bold. Yes, I know, the term scares you to death! Most of us are a bit uncomfortable with the idea of evangelism, and we get freaked out when we add the word "bold" to it. We instantly think of some crazy guy standing on a street corner waving a Bible and yelling that people are going to hell. Want to sign up for that? No, I didn't think so.

Others have mental images of Christians who wear a permanent scowl and talk incessantly about what God and the church are against. They condemn this group and despise that group. They're sure "those people" are from the devil and are ruining our country. From all appearances, they must believe scorn is one of the fruit of the Spirit.

When we look at the life of Jesus, we see something else entirely. He didn't despise people who were far from God, and He didn't blast them with threats of judgment. He graciously and lovingly moved toward people, the down-and-outers and the up-and-comers. No one was off-limits for Him. His followers were amazed that He initiated interaction with a foreign woman who was an adulterer, and at the other end of the social spectrum, people were angry that He invited himself to have dinner with a rich, hated tax collector. His love was so palpable that unbelievers longed to hang out with Him, and in those relaxed moments of sharing lives, He told them about God's love and forgiveness.

Jesus modeled how to love people into the kingdom, and He set an example we all can follow as we relate to others—no hate, no condemnation, no high-pressure tactics . . . just grace and truth. When the love of God fills us and overflows, we want to tell people about Jesus. That's what it means to be evangelistically bold.

INOCULATED

An inoculation introduces a tiny dosage of a disease that enables the body to build up an immunity so the person never suffers the full effect of the disease. I'm afraid a lot of people who come to church each week have been inoculated and never experience the fever of fervent discipleship.

When I became a Christian, I told every person who would listen about Jesus. A lot of people got saved, and I loved seeing them come to faith. It was easy to connect with unbelievers because all my friends were pagans like I'd been. Then I did something that effectively shut off the flow of evangelistic zeal and opportunities to share my faith: I joined a church. When I got involved in the life of a church, I spent virtually all my time with the members and attenders. Soon, I had very few conversations with people who weren't Christians.

When I got involved in the life of a church, I spent virtually all my time with the members and attenders. Soon, I had very few conversations with people who weren't Christians.

It gets worse. Gradually, I lost my ability to connect with outsiders. I started using language I heard in the church, I talked about things church people talked about, and I went to places where church people went. It wasn't long before I seldom even saw my old friends, and when I saw them, I was a very different person than the Dennis they'd known before!

We can't be evangelistically bold if we're relationally odd. Let's be clear: some people considered Jesus to be really odd, but it wasn't the societal outsiders. Again and again, the people who gave Him a hard time were the strict, religious people, those who were insiders and proud of it. When Jesus was in the process of calling twelve men to be His apostles, He didn't pick a single member of the religious elite. The Twelve were all regular people. In fact, He included Matthew, a tax collector who was considered a traitor by the other Jews. In his Gospel, Matthew describes that scene:

> As Jesus passed on from there, He saw a man named Matthew sitting at the tax office. And He said to him, "Follow Me." So he arose and followed Him.
>
> Now it happened, as Jesus sat at the table in the house, that behold, many tax collectors and sinners came and sat down with Him and His disciples. And when the Pharisees saw it, they said to His disciples, "Why does your Teacher eat with tax collectors and sinners?"
>
> When Jesus heard that, He said to them, "Those who are well have no need of a physician, but those who are sick. But go and learn what this means: 'I desire mercy and not sacrifice.' For I did not come to call the righteous, but sinners, to repentance." (Matthew 9:9–13)

Our experience of God's mercy compels us to extend mercy to misfits and outcasts. The Pharisees were too focused on their power, their prestige, and their purposes to care for others. They loved their religious duties and rituals more than the people Jesus came to save. They upheld their traditions, but they let down Jesus and the people He loved. It's the same for many people today: far too many of us are so completely immersed in our churches that we don't notice people outside our walls—or we notice, but we don't care enough to engage them because it requires too much of us.

Reaching out to the lost isn't just a nice idea. Jesus commanded it. Believers ignore the command, but disciples obey. Jesus told His followers, "I have been given all authority in heaven and on earth. Therefore, go and make disciples of all the nations, baptizing them in the name of the Father and the Son and the Holy Spirit. Teach these new disciples to obey all the commands I have given you. And be sure of this: I am with you always, even to the end of the age. . . . But you will receive power when the Holy Spirit comes upon you. And you will be my witnesses, telling people about me everywhere—in Jerusalem, throughout Judea, in Samaria, and to the ends of the earth" (Matthew 28:18–20; Acts 1:8, NLT). Sharing Jesus isn't optional for disciples. We may have to change some things in us and around us so we can be effective, but we'll do whatever it takes to make those changes because Jesus commands it.

To become effective witnesses, we need three things: bold love, bold influence, and bold service.

BOLD LOVE

For centuries, people who read the Bible have marveled at the love of Jesus—it wasn't the syrupy, sentimental greeting card kind of love; it was strong, sacrificial, and life-changing. When people in the world today think of Christians, do they see us as people who are known for sacrificial care for others, or do they see us as narrow, self-righteous, judgmental opponents of everything they value? When we're known for what's wrong instead of what's right, we lose our audience.

Love is the chief hallmark of a disciple. As the old song says, "They'll know we are Christians by our love." This quality of love is proven by

our willingness to step into people's lives and provide help, care,
and time, even when it's costly and
inconvenient, and even when they
don't agree with our principles and
doctrines.

Love is the chief hallmark of a disciple.

As we saw earlier, Jesus explained that the entire content of God's laws and commands in the Old Testament is summed up in four words: Love God; love people. To love the way Jesus loves means we open every part of ourselves—not just portions—to respond to the love of God by loving Him in return. Then, out of hearts overflowing with the love of God, we love the people He loves, which is every person on earth.

Why aren't most of us evangelistically bold? It's simple: because we love ourselves more than we love God and people. We live for what makes us happy and comfortable. We insulate ourselves from others by living in neighborhoods where people don't need us, and we spend time with people who don't ask much of us. We live focused on ourselves, and we seldom even touch the people across the street or in the next office. Oh, some of us give, love, and serve, but more to be noticed and applauded than for the good of the person we're "helping." On the outside, we appear selfless and noble, but we're still in the center of our lives. Am I being too harsh? Maybe, but if the shoe fits . . .

Love always requires more from us than we normally want to give. Years ago, our church had an outreach the weekend before Easter. Our small groups held cookouts and invited people to come over so would could get to know our neighbors. A lot of our groups participated, including the group Colleen and I led. A few days before the cookout, we knocked on doors to personally invite the people on our street. They may have thought we were Jehovah's Witnesses, but we assured them we just wanted them to come for dinner and a good time that Saturday evening.

The people in our group showed up on Saturday with all kinds of delicious food. Slowly, a trickle of our neighbors joined us. Many of them brought refreshments: beer and wine coolers. The party kicked off, and more people came. A lot of them started drinking . . . and they kept drinking. I was glad they felt free to be themselves. To be honest, some of the people in our small group felt a little uncomfortable at the party, but I assured them Jesus hung out with people just like this. We also discovered that our neighbors were much more open to talk about God in this environment!

During the party I talked with Dan, the father of one of my daughter's friends. We had never met before, so I was glad to get to know him. Dan asked, "Dennis, what do you do?"

When I first meet people, I try very hard to keep one fact a secret: that I'm a pastor. I've found that this word freaks people out. So when Dan asked, I was ready. I said, "I'm in the restoration business." Dan looked a bit puzzled. He probably thought I refinished furniture, so I told him, "You know, things that are broken, things that need to be made new. That's what I do."

After we talked for a while, both of us engaged in other conversations. At one point, I noticed that Dan was looking at me with an expression that clearly communicated, "Hey, I found out what you really do for a living!" I could tell he wasn't thrilled to learn I'm a pastor. It became even clearer later when I overheard him complaining about churches, pastors, and the Christian faith in general. *Everybody* heard him because he was talking so loudly. I walked over to try to smooth things out, but it was obvious he was really angry. Finally, he embarrassed himself so much that he decided to leave the party. His wife apologized as they walked out.

The next Sunday was Easter, and I preached several services. When they were over, I was both thrilled, but exhausted. After Colleen and I got home, I noticed the light flashing on our answering machine. I wanted to ignore it, but I hit the button. It was Dan's wife. She said, "Dennis, I want to apologize again for the way my husband acted at the party, but I also wanted to tell you that Dan's in the hospital." After a pause, her voice shook as she added, "He tried to kill himself last night."

She also left the name of the hospital, so I immediately told Colleen, "We have to go see him." When we arrived, Dan was in an intensive care room with his wife and daughter. He was awake, but he looked awful. It was obvious he had come very close to success in his attempt. He saw us and asked, "What are you doing here?"

I said, "We found out you were in the hospital, and we wanted to come by to see you."

His eyes welled up, and he told me sadly, "Nobody else in the neighborhood has come. You're the only one."

I didn't preach to him, and I didn't make a big deal about being there. Colleen and I just wanted to be there with him and his family in their hour of need.

A few weeks later, a friend called to offer me four tickets to a Braves game he was unable to attend. I gladly accepted and then thought about who I might invite to go with me. I considered some friends in the church, but suddenly the Lord said, "Why do you automatically think of them? Why don't you take somebody who needs Jesus?"

Well, it wasn't hard to figure out who that might be. I called Dan to invite him and his daughter to go with my daughter and me—a dad-dy-daughter double date. When we arrived at the stadium, we were all excited, but then a baseball game broke out. I love baseball, but it's not the most thrilling game in the world. In the second inning, Dan decided to have a beer. He had another one in each of the next six innings. During lulls in the action (which are almost constant in baseball games), I told Dan about Jesus. He wasn't defiant or defensive like he had been a few weeks before at the party. He listened (as well as he could).

Another few weeks went by until one Sunday morning I gave an invitation for people to trust in Christ and come forward. A lot of people came to the altar. I went down the line to pray with each one. About halfway, I found Dan standing with his wife and daughter. I prayed with all of them, and then Dan told me, "Dennis, I can't get over the extravagant love you've shown me. You didn't ditch me when I was so rude to you at your party, and you didn't condemn me when I had a few too many beers at the ballgame. Over the past few weeks, I've realized I've gotten far from God. I wouldn't have known Jesus if He had appeared with a red hat on, but you showed Jesus to me. That's why I'm here today."

I didn't do anything extraordinary. I was just available to let the love of Jesus flow through me, and His love is extravagant. Real evangelism isn't complex; it's simply loving people enough to move into their lives, even when it's costly. Jesus laid down His life for us, and in little ways, we lay down our lives for others.

You'll be amazed at what happens when you love boldly.

BOLD INFLUENCE

What does bold love look like? Jesus used two powerful metaphors to illustrate our identity as His people and our impact on those around us. He spoke to a crowd:

> "You are the salt of the earth. But what good is salt if it has lost its flavor? Can you make it salty again? It will be thrown out and trampled underfoot as worthless. You are the light of the world—like a city on a hilltop that cannot be hidden. No one lights a lamp and then puts it under a basket. Instead, a lamp is placed on a stand, where it gives light to everyone in the house. In the same way, let your good deeds shine out for all to see, so that everyone will praise your heavenly Father." (Matthew 5:13–16, NLT)

Salt and light . . . that's how we influence people. God wants us to be flavorful and colorful, not drab and bland. The ancient world didn't have refrigerators, so the only way to preserve meat was to cure it with salt. In that climate meat spoiled within a few hours, so curing it was essential. We still do that today with "salt cured pork" and a few other meats, but it's rare.

But salt does more than preserve meat; it also gives it flavor. Cooks know the importance of salt in almost every dish. It makes every food more delicious. For disciples of Jesus, the first role of salt is obvious: the gospel of grace is the only preservative that keeps people from experiencing the wrath of God and eternal alienation we deserve because of our sins. But the second role isn't as obvious. When we interact with people, what flavor do they experience? Do they say, "Man, that's delicious! I want more of that"? Do they think, "Hmmm. Not much flavor there. I think I'll move on to something tastier"? Or do they wince, "Blech! That's disgusting"?

I'm not only talking about their responses when we share the gospel with them. I'm also referring to our normal, everyday interactions. Do we leave them hungry for more, or do they look for something that tastes better?

Jesus also said we are lights to the people around us. Again, light has two benefits: it illuminates reality so people can see clear to make good decisions, and it makes beautiful things more visible, vibrant, and attractive. Jesus said we are to shine like a city on a hill so everyone in the surrounding countryside can see the source of our light. In personal relationships, we don't hide our light under a bowl of pride, self-pity, fear, or resentment. Instead, we put it on a stand so people can thrive in the love, forgiveness, acceptance, and power of the Spirit. In the darkness, even the loveliest flower or painting or person goes unnoticed, but in the light, the brilliant colors and beauty pop out and amaze people.

If we're born again, God has put His light in us. Is it shining, or is it

If we're born again, God has put His light in us. Is it shining, or is it hidden?

hidden? Does it reveal the reality of sin and grace so people can make good decisions about God, and does it show the beauty of Christ—all He is, all He has done, and all He has planned for each of us?

Let me get in your kitchen for a minute. Many Christians think social media is the perfect platform to spout all kinds of crazy and offensive messages. They "like" or retweet (or compose) conspiracy theories that have no basis in reality, and they spout vile comments about political leaders or celebrities they don't like. I don't know who's worse, left wing liberals or right wing conservatives. I've seen incredibly hateful, offensive messages from Christians on both sides.

Paul used the analogy of salt near the end of his letter to the Colossians. He reminded them, "Walk in wisdom toward those who are outside, redeeming the time. Let your speech always be with grace, seasoned with salt, that you may know how you ought to answer each one" (Colossians 4:5-6)

What do our unbelieving "friends" think when they see and read our posts? What flavor do they taste? Is it the sweet and salty flavor of God's wisdom, love, and kindness, or is it the bitter poison of racism, xenophobia, bitter partisanship, and wild-eyed fanaticism? Do we delight in condemning those who disagree with us, or can we engage with them in thoughtful, loving dialogue to win their hearts to Jesus? (I don't see much thoughtful, loving dialogue on social media, but occasionally I find links to wonderful articles.)

Here's what I'm asking you to do: Think, people! Evaluate the flavor and color of your spoken and written messages, and make changes. Some of you need to get off social media until God works in your heart to give you a love for those who disagree with you. Jesus died for His enemies. What are you willing to sacrifice to love people whose opinions differ from yours?

Our lives broadcast messages everywhere we go. Our words, our clothes, and even our cars communicate with those around us. One man who attended our church got really excited about Jesus, and he wanted to find a way to tell others about his new joy. He had a custom bumper sticker made, and he proudly put it on his car. He came early every Sunday so he could park in the most conspicuous spot. As people walked in with their children, they looked at his car and read: "Victory World Church— Kicking the Devil's A_ _ Every Sunday"! Now, I appreciate the sentiment, although that's not a message we want to communicate to the kids who are learning to read.

The world tells people to "let it all hang out" and "don't let anyone tell you what to say or do." Believers still have a foot in both worlds, so they feel conflicted about Jesus' instructions to be salt and light, but disciples know better. They realize every interaction, every response on social media, and every attitude toward leaders either adds a delicious flavor or is putrid. Our messages either reveal beautiful colors or pull down the shade so the love of God remains in darkness. We have a powerful influence on the people around us—for good or ill.

BOLD SERVICE

Bold love and bold influence always show up in bold service. This shouldn't surprise us. Jesus, the Creator, King, and Savior, "emptied himself" of His privileges to become a servant. He didn't just give up a little time and convenience; He gave up His reputation and His life.

His life was no longer about his own power and prestige, but about the wonder of Jesus' power and compassion.

He didn't come to be served, but to serve. And He wants us to follow in His footsteps. Paul had been an angry, power-hungry, vindictive leader, but when Jesus met him on the Road to Damascus, God's love melted Paul's heart. His life was no longer about his own power and prestige, but about the wonder of Jesus' power and compassion.

When we read Luke's account of the early church in Acts, we see the extent to which Paul was willing to become a servant so everyone could hear and respond to the gospel. The Corinthians were a contentious bunch. Like the disciples at the Last Supper, they argued about who was the greatest among them. In Paul's letter he attempted to correct their thinking and attitudes by explaining that being a servant was central to his calling . . . and to the role of every person who follows Christ. He was willing to do anything—anything!—to convince people to respond to the gospel. He explained how much he was willing to suffer to tell people about Jesus:

It seems to me that God has put us who bear his Message on stage in a theater in which no one wants to buy a ticket. We're something everyone stands around and stares at, like an accident in the street. We're the Messiah's misfits. You might be sure of yourselves, but we live in the midst of frailties and uncertainties. You might be well-thought-of by others, but we're mostly kicked around. Much of the time we don't have enough to eat, we wear patched and threadbare clothes, we get doors slammed in our faces, and we pick up odd jobs anywhere we can to eke out a living. When they call us names, we say, "God bless you." When they spread rumors about *us*, we put in a good word for *them*. We're treated like garbage, potato peelings from the culture's kitchen. And it's not getting any better. (1 Corinthians 4:9–13 MSG)

Paul was willing to pay a high price to serve boldly. Believers look at the cost of serving others, and they conclude, "Hmmm. I'm not sure it's worth it." Disciples recognize the price that has to be paid to enter the lives of lost people and love them into the kingdom, and they conclude, "Yeah, I want in!"

We often get the order of events backward. We start off telling people the gospel, and we hope they respond so we can have a relationship with them. Their faith is, in effect, their ticket to moving forward with us. But that's not what we see in the model of Jesus, Paul, and others who are servants. Their starting point is serving people. After we've proven our love, people are much more receptive to the message of the gospel. Of course, even if we serve amazingly well, there's no guarantee they'll trust in Christ. Jesus was the ultimate servant, and they killed Him! (How's that for encouragement?) But serving people is the first step in evangelism.

Years ago, my friend Dave Nowak and his wife bought a house in a quaint, older neighborhood in Decatur, Georgia. Dave has been a pastor on our staff for many years, but at the time he was just starting the process of learning to be a disciple of Christ—and he learned in a hurry! After they moved in, they realized the area of the city had become a hotspot for the gay community. A number of gay couples bought houses on their street, including two men who moved in next door. Dave went over to introduce himself, and he was determined to become their friend. They often had parties, but Dave and his family weren't aware of what was going on because they would cover the windows with black tarp paper.

Dave tried to connect with them at every opportunity. He talked to them about their careers, and he helped them with projects around their house. They knew he was a Christian, but he wasn't like the stereotypical judgmental Christians who have only condemning words for gays. After a couple of years, one of his neighbors told Dave that his partner had contracted HIV-AIDS. At that time the prognosis was grim because effective drugs had not been developed to combat the disease. Instead of avoiding the men, Dave became even more involved at that point. He cut their grass, trimmed their bushes, and brought them food. One day the sick man asked Dave, "Man, why are you doing all this for me?"

Dave just smiled and said, "Jesus has been kind to me. This is the least I can do for you."

Before his sick neighbor died, Dave led him to Christ.

There was a time in the church when helping people was literally a matter of life and death. Historians tell us that two plagues ravaged the Roman world in the second and third centuries. Each time, between a quarter and a third of the entire population perished. The first plague began in 165 and may have been a smallpox epidemic. In fact, Emperor Marcus Aurelius was one of the plague's victims. The second plague, which may have been measles, devastated the empire beginning in 251.

In each of these times of dread disease, the pagans prayed to their gods, but people kept dying. They looked to their doctors for help, but the doctors were leaving town to save their own lives. Family members fled from their homes and left infected brothers, sisters, parents, and children to die. Without basic nursing care, most of those who contracted the diseases died horrible deaths.

The Christians, though, didn't run out on their families. They stayed and nursed them, and they went to the houses of the pagans to care for them, too. Dionysius, a leader in the church, described their motivation:

Most of our brother Christians showed unbounded love and loyalty, never sparing themselves and thinking only of one another. Heedless of danger, they took charge of the sick, attending to their every need and ministering to them in Christ, and with them departed this life serenely happy; for they were infected by others with the disease, drawing on themselves the sickness of their neighbors and cheerfully accepting their pains. Many, in nursing and curing others, transferred their death to themselves and died in their stead. . . . The best of our brothers lost their lives in this manner.[8]

These compassionate Christians reached out to help "the least of these." They loved their sick neighbors as themselves, and God used them to save the lives of thousands of people. They served at the risk of their own lives and in fact, many of them died caring for their neighbors.

In *The Rise of Christianity*, Rodney Stark concluded that the bold service of the Christians during those two plagues caused the number of believers to rapidly increase in the Roman Empire. How? Christians cared for their own family members instead of leaving them to die, so their mortality rate was much lower. And the Romans, whose lives were saved by the selfless service of their Christian neighbors, became very receptive to the gospel because they saw Christ's love in action! Within two hundred years, the number of Christians in the Roman Empire grew from less than one percent to more than twenty-five percent. Christianity eventually became the dominant faith of the Empire. According to Stark, Christianity spread throughout the Roman world because Jesus' disciples risked their lives to serve sick people around them.[9]

PAIN OR PLEASURE

Does telling people about Jesus seem like a weight around your neck, or does your love for God and for people naturally (and supernaturally) motivate you to interact with those you meet each day? Certainly, we can benefit from training in how to communicate the gospel message clearly and effectively, but that's not the problem for most Christians. Training is an easy hurdle to cross. The real issue is deeper: Is God's grace truly amazing to us, or is the Christian faith still just a bunch of do's, don'ts, and have-to's? When we experience the love of God to the extent that we're "filled to all the fullness of God," we won't be driven by guilt or fear. We'll be compelled by the love of God to reach out to care for the people around us.

In the formative years of the church, Christians were persecuted, and they had to flee from their homes. As refugees, they didn't wallow in self-pity and resentment for all they had left behind. They saw themselves as missionaries. They may have lost their homes and earthly possessions, but they had a treasure they wanted to share with everyone who would listen.

Today, we aren't threatened the way they were. We have far more stability, more rights, and more possessions. What are we doing with them? As Jesus said to disciples then and now, "To whom much is given, much is required."

THINK ABOUT IT:

1. What percentage of your time do you spend around Christians, and what percent with unbelievers? How many unbelievers would call you a good friend? Are you satisfied with those numbers? Is God satisfied? Why or why not?

2. What are some ways we can keep our language and lifestyles from being "too churchy"?

3. Think of someone you know who isn't a believer. What would it look like for you to really love that person?

4. To what extent is your life flavorful and colorful—or flavorless and colorless—to unbelievers? Explain your answer.

5. How have you seen Christians present themselves on social media? How do you communicate on these platforms? How should disciples communicate on them?

6. What are some excuses believers use to keep from selflessly serving those who don't know Christ? What are some reasons disciples serve with humility and joy?

7. On a scale of 0 (zip) to 10 (fully), how evangelistically bold are you? Explain your answer. What needs to improve?

CHAPTER 8

A DISCIPLE . . .
ENGAGES IN BIBLICAL COMMUNITY

I n our world today, we have more information in our pockets than people a generation ago dreamed of having in the biggest city's library, and we have connections with more people than we can count . . . but most of them are superficial. We have few meaningful relationships.

Who are your best friends . . . the people who know you best and whose minds you can often read? Some of the people on my list I've known since I was a little boy; others have become close friends in the last few years.

What constitutes a true friend? Think of the people you might include in this category, and then consider the following questions:

- How often do you have heart-to-heart talks?

- How frequently do each of you share your hopes and fears, your victories and struggles?

- How often do you ask to be held accountable to do something hard?

- What real impact are you having on each other?

- When you're together, are both of you becoming disciples, or remaining believers?

If we're honest, many (maybe most) of us would have to admit we don't have people like this in our lives. Our friendships don't go this deep, so they're not very encouraging or challenging. Actually, we may prefer to keep them that way because we'd rather not risk being known, being vulnerable, or being uncomfortable. They're friends, and we want to keep them as friends, even if the friendship is only an inch deep.

TENSION

We've already seen that the church in Corinth was a mess. Paul had to write a blunt, corrective letter to set them straight. They were believers, but they certainly weren't acting like disciples!

We often read the thirteenth chapter of 1 Corinthians at weddings. It's about love, and everybody sighs because "it's so sweet." I have to tell you, though, that's not the response of the first people who read this letter! In the previous chapters of this letter, Paul didn't pull any punches, and in 1 Corinthians 13, a masterpiece about God's love, Paul nails them to the wall.

The Corinthians had spiritual experiences, but without caring for others. They had amazing gifts, but they were proud. They gave and sacrificed, but to be noticed and applauded. Paul explained the nature of love in terms he had used to rebuke them earlier in the letter. He told them love is patient because they had been so impatient; he reminded them love is kind because they had been harsh; he proclaimed that love doesn't envy because they were eaten alive with jealousy. You get the picture.

The believers in Corinth didn't look any different from the pagans in their city, so in his follow-up letter, Paul continued to correct them. He wrote:

Do not be unequally yoked together with unbelievers. For what fellowship has righteousness with lawlessness? And what communion has light with darkness? And what accord has Christ with Belial? Or what part has a believer with an unbeliever? And what agreement has the temple of God with idols? For you are the temple of the living God. As God has said:

"I will dwell in them
And walk among them.
I will be their God,
And they shall be My people."

Therefore

"Come out from among them
And be separate, says the Lord.
Do not touch what is unclean,
And I will receive you."
"I will be a Father to you,
And you shall be My sons and daughters,
Says the Lord Almighty."
(2 Corinthians 6:14–18)

In the previous chapter, we saw that God wants us to penetrate the culture like salt to provide preservative and flavor, and we're to be lights to bring truth into the darkness around us. But here God says to remain separate from the culture. What's the deal?

As it is with many other aspects of discipleship, we need wisdom to live in the tension between two worlds. Like Jesus, we are to be friends with unbelievers so we can earn the right to be heard when we share the gospel with them, and like Jesus, we keep our hearts pure from the stain of sin and the shadow of darkness. It's not one or the other; it's both.

When I became a Christian, all of my friends were unbelievers. I was loyal to my friends, and I had no intention of leaving them. However, as

I drew closer to God and read the Bible, I realized I had changed, and as a result my relationships needed to change. My loyalties were no longer with my old friends. My chief loyalty was to God, His kingdom, and His people. I still had the same friends, but I was no longer "yoked" to them. When a young ox was yoked to a mature one, the young one went wherever the old one went. When we trust Jesus, we change yokes. We're no longer yoked to our old friends and our previous way of life. We're now yoked to Christ, and we follow Him wherever He leads.

His life was no longer about his own power and prestige, but about the wonder of Jesus' power and compassion.

In recent decades, I've concluded that the number one reason people remain believers and fail to become disciples is the fact they are still yoked to their previous relationships. They may show up in church and sing the songs, but their deepest loyalties haven't changed. They keep listening to the same people, so they keep living by the same values.

Our relationships are the air we breathe and the water we swim in. Our human connections shape our lives more than we can imagine. People in the Roman world in the first century understood the importance of relationships, but not us. Those of us who have grown up in America have western individualism ingrained in us. We're fiercely independent, and we believe we can make it on our own. The first-century Christians—and most of the world today, especially in Asia, Africa, and Latin America—have a different view: we are only as strong as our most important human connections.

The Bible tells us that God gathers His people to create a new kind of community. The dictionary defines community as "a group of people leading a common life according to a rule." A rule is a guiding principle, a common interest, an energy-generating factor. For years, the common interests of our communities have been school, sports, music, work, and family. In the kingdom of God, our common interests are Christ and His kingdom—not our socioeconomic status, our part of town, our nationality, or the color of our skin, but the love, power, and purposes of Jesus. This makes us radically different than any other community on the planet.

SMALL ENOUGH TO LOVE ENOUGH

One day in the fourth decade of the first century, something remarkable happened. The Feast of Pentecost brought people to Jerusalem from all over the known world. Their clothes, languages, and foods were different from each other. Yet when the Holy Spirit fell on the 120 who had gathered for prayer, they miraculously spoke the gospel in languages all the people from those nations could understand. Luke tells us, "On that day about three thousand believed [Peter's] message and were baptized. They spent their time learning from the apostles, and they were like family to each other. They also broke bread and prayed together" (Acts 2:41–42, CEV).

Notice what happened to very diverse people when the Spirit captured their hearts: they spent time learning, they were like family, they ate together, and they prayed together. No matter what differences had divided them before, the Spirit united them.

Luke went on to provide a detailed description of this new community. In the following days, their unity didn't collapse into bickering; it grew even stronger: "Everyone was amazed by the many miracles and wonders that the apostles worked. All the Lord's followers often met together, and they shared everything they had. They would sell their property and possessions and give the money to whoever needed it. Day after day they met together in the temple. They broke bread together in different homes and shared their food happily and freely, while praising God. Everyone liked them, and each day the Lord added to their group others who were being saved" (Acts 2:43–47, CEV).

Doesn't that sound attractive to you? If so, you're definitely on the path to become a disciple! When Colleen and I lived in Richmond and were dating, the pastor of our church asked for volunteers to host a small group. I was willing to do anything for Jesus, so I eagerly agreed to host, even though I wasn't far along in my faith to be the spiritual leader. The leader of our group was Pete, an African-American man who became my friend and mentor. This was my first venture into a genuine, Acts 2, multiethnic community, and I loved it. I began to learn some valuable lessons from Pete, and those lessons are the foundation for every biblical community.

IN A BIBLICAL COMMUNITY, PEOPLE LEARN TO VALUE EACH OTHER

In almost every church, you'll find three kinds of people: the haves, the have-nots, and the sort-of-haves. The haves complain about paying taxes that benefit the have-nots. The have-nots complain that the haves aren't paying enough taxes to take care of people like them. The sort-of-haves side with one or the other, depending on whom they're with at the time. If you look closely at the groupings in the lobby of most churches before and after services, you'll find haves hanging out with haves, have-nots with have-nots, and the sort-of-haves hovering in between.

As we read the first chapters of Acts, we see all three kinds of people in the early church, but they loved each other instead of criticizing one another. They trusted each other instead of being mutually suspicious. They looked beyond the differences of nationality, wealth, and status, and they valued each other as members of God's family.

Years ago when I wrote our church's "core values," the first four came very easily, but one really challenged me. God told me this one should be: Value all people the same way Jesus values them.

Jesus doesn't care how much money you have, if there are letters after your name, what you wear, where you live, or if you're in prison. He doesn't care where you've come from or what you've done. You are His beloved child, His delight, His treasure.

When God's people despaired because they had messed up so badly they were sure God had abandoned them, God tenderly assured them: "Can a mother forget the baby at her breast and have no compassion on the child she has borne? Though she may forget, I will not forget you! See, I have engraved you on the palms of my hands; your walls are ever before me" (Isaiah 49:15–16, NIV).

God has your name tattooed on His hand! That's how much He values each of His children. If I'm a disciple, I'll learn to value His children in the same way—I'll treasure them.

> If I'm a disciple, I'll learn to value His children in the same way—I'll treasure them.

That doesn't mean I have to agree with them about politics or music or cultural tastes, but it means I love them enough to look beyond the secondary things to focus on the primary thing: loving each other the way God loves each of us.

This principle blows out the sides of our rigid boxes. We no longer include or exclude people based on meaningless criteria such as race, origin, gender, political persuasion, or financial status. Ancient hatreds have to die, and new loves must be established in their place. The family of God may have some disagreements, but we must not major on the minors and let our differences divide us. Unity isn't just a nice concept—it's God's grand design that demonstrates His love and power to a desperate world.

IN A BIBLICAL COMMUNITY, PEOPLE LEARN TO BE AUTHENTIC WITH EACH OTHER

Poser. That's what we call people who hide who they really are and present a false identity . . . always to impress. Now, don't get me wrong. There's nothing wrong with wanting to look presentable. I'm all for clean clothes and makeup! But I've seen people post profile pictures on Facebook that were taken twenty years ago, when the men had hair and the women were . . . oh, never mind.

People grow spiritually only to the level they're open and honest about their hopes and dreams, their fears and doubts—and the secrets they've hidden for years. Trusting people with the things we've buried in our hearts is one of the most challenging steps in becoming Christ's disciple, but it's essential.

Still, we don't need to be stupid. In Alcoholics Anonymous, people who get to Step 5 are asked to tell a trustworthy person what they discovered in Step 4 when they made "a searching and fearless moral inventory" of their lives. Most people in the AA program will tell you this conversation is the turning point in their recovery. Speaking the truth about their deepest, darkest secrets is liberating, but also terrifying, so they have to be judicious about whom they tell. They find someone who has been in the program longer, and grown wiser, and has become a sponsor to those who are just beginning to be honest about the craziness in their lives.

When we provide a safe, supportive environment—for an individual, a couple, or a small group—amazing things can happen. Not long after we started our first small group at my apartment in Richmond, two young women came and asked if they could join. We were glad to have them. In the middle of a discussion about a passage of Scripture, one of them raised her hand. The leader stopped the conversation and smiled at her. She said, "I want to tell you something. It doesn't really pertain to what we're talking about, but I think you need to know it anyway. We started coming to the church a few weeks ago, and we really feel welcome there. But you need to know that we're gay." She waited a second or two for this news to sink in, and then she continued, "We fell in love, and we've lived together for the last four years. We want to go to church, but I'm sure everyone assumes we're just good friends. We're more than that . . . a lot more than that."

When no one got up and walked out, and no one told them they were going to hell, I think she felt relieved. She then surprised us when she continued, "We've started reading the Bible, and we've realized our life-style doesn't line up with what God teaches about love and marriage. We believe God has led us to this church, and God has led us to this group, to help us make a decision about the future of our relationship. We want to follow God, but we're really confused. We don't know what to do with our feelings and our commitment to each other, and now with our commitment to God. Will you help us?"

I didn't say a word, but I was thinking, *Oh, man, nobody told me this was going to happen when I opened the door to have a group in my apartment! I thought we were just going to be a bunch of nice people eating nice food and saying nice things to each other!*

Before anyone could respond, another young woman blurted out, "Since we're being honest, I need to let you know that I've been sleeping with my boyfriend. I know it's wrong, but I don't want to lose him." In the next half hour, people told each other about things I never imagined anyone would say out loud. Those people loved each other and supported each other, so much that they were willing to be authentic with each other. It was fertile soil for people to see God work in dramatic ways—in all our lives.

It's not that way in many churches and small groups. Instead of being authentic, we hide, we tell white lies, and in many creative ways we avoid telling the truth. All of us are sinners. The question isn't whether we sin, but what we do with our sin. Will we allow the light of God to shine on both our actions and the motives that prompted them, or will we hide from each other and try to hide from God? When Adam and Eve sinned, they covered themselves in fig leaves to hide their shame. Did they think the Creator of the universe couldn't see under the leaves? Do we think the same Creator can't see beneath our posing and hiding?

> We put on the face of a happy, competent, self-assured person, and we try to keep all the mess below the surface. It's like trying to hold a bunch of balloons under water. It's constant and exhausting work!

Many of us spend an inordinate amount of time and energy managing our images. Instead of responding to the Holy Spirit's whisper (or shout) that we've sinned, confessing our sin and experiencing the cleansing of God's forgiveness and restoration, we live like gangsters hiding from the law. We put on the face of a happy, competent, self-assured person, and we try to keep all the mess below the surface. It's like trying to hold a bunch of balloons under water. It's constant and exhausting work!

The Bible has a word for people who refuse God's encouragement to be honest: hypocrite. We say one thing and do another; we present an identity but hide who we really are. Jesus used this word as He exposed the truth about self-righteous religious leaders. They were proud of their external righteousness, but they didn't care about the people God loves. Jesus didn't try to be gentle when He told them, "You hypocrites! Isaiah was right when he prophesied about you: 'These people honor me with their lips, but their hearts are far from me'" (Matthew 15:7–8, NIV).

We sing inspirational songs, say the right religious words, and smile, but we're rude to our spouses, harsh with our kids, negligent in caring for people, and dishonest at work. I've seen couples with their kids yelling and snarling at each other in the parking lot, but as soon as the car door opens, they are the picture of a happy family. I'm not recommending that people yell and snarl at each other while they're in worship, but I'm suggesting they deal with their hurt and anger before and after they come to church! The church doesn't exist for perfect people, but for those who are humble enough to admit they desperately need the love and power of God.

Hypocrisy is the internal reason people aren't authentic, but sometimes we find another external reason: many have been the targets of harsh criticism from self-righteous believers, and they don't ever want to be exposed to that kind of abuse again. In the family of God, our relationships are to be characterized by kindness as well as truth. Jesus was very clear about how gentle we should be with others: "Why do you look at the speck in your brother's eye, but do not perceive the plank in your own eye? Or how can you say to your brother, 'Brother, let me remove the speck that is in your eye,' when you yourself do not see the plank that is in your own eye? Hypocrite! First remove the plank from your own eye, and then you will see clearly to remove the speck that is in your brother's eye" (Luke 6:41–42).

If we don't realize we have planks in our own eyes—that is, that we're sinners in need of God's forgiveness—we'll be quick and harsh in our condemnation of others we consider unacceptable and unsavory. How many times does a person have to be treated with contempt before he or she is reluctant to be vulnerable with others? Not very many!

Jesus was incredibly patient with people, and He was a master at showing people their sin so they could experience forgiveness. When a woman was caught in adultery and thrown in front of Jesus, the religious leaders demanded that He condemn her, but He challenged her accusers, "He who is without sin among you, let him throw a stone at her first" (John 8:7). They all walked away.

When the Pharisees stood around Jesus and a group of sinners to express contempt that He would be friends with such rabble, Jesus told three parables about a lost sheep, a lost coin, and a lost son. In the first two stories, someone went out to find the sheep and the coin, but no one looked for the lost son to bring him home. Everyone understood that Jesus was calling out the Pharisees for their lack of love for lost people. They should have been making friends with the prostitutes and tax collectors instead of standing back and condemning them.

Peter's denial of Jesus after His arrest shattered the proud man's heart. He didn't have to be convinced he was a sinner. Instead, he had to be convinced Jesus hadn't given up on him. After the shock of the cross and the resurrection, Peter left Jerusalem and went back to his old profession of fishing. After a long night with no fish, Peter saw a man standing on the shore and realized it was Jesus. He flung himself into the water and swam to Him. On the beach, Jesus gently and lovingly asked Peter three times, "Do you love me?" Jesus was giving Peter the opportunity to affirm his love as many times as he had denied Him—and Peter became the leader of the new church.

The point is that nothing we think, say, or do is outside the view of Almighty God. He has proven His love for us, so we can be completely honest with Him. Our honesty and our healing, though, are always in the context of God's family. We belong to God, and we belong to each other. Authenticity is the path to emotional, spiritual, and relational healing. James tells us, "Confess your sins to each other and pray for each other so that you may be healed. The earnest prayer of a righteous person has great power and produces wonderful results" (James 5:16, NLT).

IN A BIBLICAL COMMUNITY, PEOPLE ARE ACCOUNTABLE TO EACH OTHER

When we're involved in each other's lives, we aren't afraid to encourage people to "excel still more," and we aren't shy about asking hard questions. We want people to thrive. We listen when they share their dreams, and we help them construct plans to reach those dreams. When they struggle with a bad attitude, a habitual sin, or a troubled relationship, we provide support and accountability.

Near the end of his epic letter to the Romans, Paul prays, "Now may the God of patience and comfort grant you to be like-minded toward one another, according to Christ Jesus, that you may with one mind and one mouth glorify the God and Father of our Lord Jesus Christ" (Romans 15:56).

We are channels of God's love and strength. As God pours His endurance and encouragement into us, we can then pour them into others so that all of us glorify the Lord. That's the nature of powerful, accountable relationships in the body of Christ.

I've often been grateful for the help of others who have stepped in to hold me accountable to my commitment to be Christ's disciple. When Colleen and I started dating, we were committed to not having sex before marriage, but we weren't sure how far we should go in our physical relationship. All either of us had known before was to let lust reign, so we were novices at self-control. We talked with a couple who lived near us, and they agreed to ask us hard questions about our relationship. They explained the nature of lust and the power of previous habits. They said we'd need to be both wise and strong if wanted to avoid giving in to the lust of the flesh. They advised us to avoid being alone in places where intimacy would come easily. During those unguarded moments, powerful feelings can overwhelm previous commitments.

As I listened to their wisdom, I thought, *I'm a 23-year-old, athletic, strapping young man. I have strong desires!* But I also realized, *If I don't get some help, those strong desires will ruin my relationship with Colleen before it gets started!*

This dear couple met with us regularly. They asked us questions, and we asked them questions. They explained that regardless of one's sexual history, it's important for a couple to have a season of purity before marriage. This proves they can trust each other. After many years of talking with people in troubled marriages, I've realized the wisdom of this couple: the lack of trust caused by sex before marriage is often a major problem.

> Believers who want to be disciples need to identify pressure points in their lives where they're vulnerable to drift into sin.

Believers who want to be disciples need to identify pressure points in their lives where they're vulnerable to drift into sin. Sex is a common issue, but people can also become preoccupied with greed, power, bitterness, out-of-control spending, shame, or something else. They may have wrestled for years with an addiction, and they need help to overcome it. Most people who attend church are believers, not disciples. They avoid accountability rather than welcome it, so they continue to struggle alone with sins and doubts.

IN A BIBLICAL COMMUNITY, PEOPLE LEARN TO CARE FOR ONE ANOTHER

People were amazed at the truth Jesus taught about God and His purposes because His teaching was far more authoritative than the rigid legalism of the religious leaders. But they were just as amazed by the

tender care He showed to people in need. He pushed past the social ta-
boos of His day to touch lepers, interact with foreigners, comfort those
who were sick and blind, have meals with tax collectors, and befriend
pimps and prostitutes. Even more stunning: those people genuinely enjoyed being with Him!

Nothing speaks louder about our connection to Jesus than our love
for the people around us. One day I received a call to let me know a young
woman in our church had suffered a stroke. When I arrived at the hospital, about a dozen members of our church were in her room. I wondered
how they got there first.

I guess they noticed that I looked a little surprised because one lady
whispered, "Pastor Dennis, we're in the same small group together. We're
going to see her and her family through all this." Instantly I thought, *This is
what the church is supposed to look like!* The woman was in a coma, but the
people in that room were committed to meet her every need. They took
turns staying at the hospital with her, and even took care of her children
and house.

When the church began on Pentecost, 3000 people responded to
Peter's message and joined God's family. But no one can care for that
many people, so they formed small groups where they could love one another, support one another, teach one another, and care for one another.

Some people find excuses to stay out of a small group: They're too
busy, they don't live nearby, they don't know the Bible well enough and
are afraid they'll be embarrassed, their kids have a game that night every
week, and on and on. Christians can be believers and not be intimately
involved in a caring, supportive community, but they won't become disciples. It is an environment where everyone plays a vital role. One person
may be the leader, but everyone is a pastor to pray for the others and meet
their needs.

In times of crisis, we find out how independent we really are—or not.
Sometimes people have come to me with a look of deep disappointment

and said, "Pastor, I was in the hospital, but you didn't come to see me. Where were you when I needed you?"

I tell them, "I'm so sorry, but I didn't know. No one told me you were sick. Didn't the people in your group come to see you?"

Almost always, they say, "Well, Pastor Dennis, I'm not in a group."

I want to then ask, "Do you think I'm clairvoyant?" But I don't. I just say, "I think you'd really benefit from being in a small group. Find one near you and join it. That's how we care for one another at our church."

IN A BIBLICAL COMMUNITY, PEOPLE LEARN TO SHARE THEIR POSSESSIONS

Sharing is a foreign concept for many Americans. Oh, they expect the government to redistribute wealth so people at the bottom of the economic ladder can climb a little higher, but when it comes to personal property, they have a very different perspective. Some individuals buy guns and ammo, stock up on nonperishable foods, and prepare to protect what they have against any and all comers! And a lot of those people are Christians.

In the early church, the disciples had open hearts and open wallets. As we've seen: "All the Lord's followers often met together, and they shared everything they had. They would sell their property and possessions and give the money to whoever needed it" (Acts 2:44–45, CEV). What in the world would prompt them to be so generous? They had been filled with God's generous gift of grace, so sharing their possessions felt completely good, right, and normal.

Too often today, our attention is focused on having the next great gadget. We don't want to be left behind, so we upgrade as soon as we can. We get a better phone, a nicer car, a bigger apartment or house, and finer clothes. Each purchase is only a minute, incremental expense, but the net effect is that we're always living on the edge of debt . . . or buried under it. So we worry. We can't stop thinking about two things: getting the next thing we want and finding a way to pay this month's minimum on the credit card. Sharing with others is the last thing on our minds!

The nature of spiritual life is that we're blessed so we can be a blessing. When the grace of Jesus fills our hearts, we stop being takers, and we become givers. And when we're thrilled with all God has given and done and poured into us, we love to give to others. With full hearts and open hands, we share what God has given us. In the early church and in the lives of disciples today, the compelling motivation is: whatever I have is yours.

Believers who want to be disciples need to identify pressure points in their lives where they're vulnerable to drift into sin.

Our open hearts, though, are no reason to act foolishly. If someone is genuinely in need, we gladly "bear one another's burdens, and so fulfill the law of Christ" (Galatians 6:2). But if someone is counting on our generosity to avoid being responsible, loving that person means saying, "No, it won't help you for me to bail you out." We love both the responsible and the irresponsible, but we help them in very different ways.

TAKE THE PLUNGE

The writer to the Hebrews reminds us: "Let us hold fast the confession of our hope without wavering, for He who promised is faithful. And let us consider one another in order to stir up love and good works, not forsaking the assembling of ourselves together, as is the manner of some, but exhorting one another, and so much the more as you see the Day approaching" (Hebrews 10:23–24).

When you are part of a thriving biblical community, you're far more likely to grow into a dynamic disciple of Jesus Christ. Going to church on Sunday morning is important, but connecting with other disciples during the week is even more important. Interaction with others adds depth to your understanding and specifics to your application of truth. When you are part of a vibrant biblical community, worship on Sunday morning becomes more meaningful because you're listening more intently and you're more in tune with the Spirit.

No excuses, no delays. Find a group that's committed to turning believers into disciples, and dive in with all you've got.

THINK ABOUT IT:

1. Read Acts 2:43–47. What do you imagine it was like to live in that kind of community? Is that way of living attractive to you? Why or why not?

2. Who are some people (groups or individuals) you find difficult to value the way Jesus values them? (Write in code, please!) What needs to happen in your heart to increase your genuine concern for them?

3. What are some reasons people are afraid of authenticity? Which of those reasons are legitimate, or at least understandable? Explain your answer.

4. Have you ever asked someone to hold you accountable? If so, how did it help you? If not, why not?

5. If you got gravely sick today and were rushed to the hospital, who would know? Who would come to see you? Who would take care of your needs for you? Who would you do these things for?

6. How do the weight of debt and the preoccupation with having more stuff impede our desire and ability to share what we have?

7. On a scale of 0 (none) to 10 (all the way), how committed are you to engage in biblical community? Explain your answer. What needs to change to increase your desire?

CHAPTER 9

A DISCIPLE IS . . .
JUST AND GENEROUS

M ore. Bigger. Faster. Most of us are never satisfied because we keep reaching for the next level of comfort, power, fun, and prestige . . . and then when we reach it, we realize we still long for more. The cycle of reaching, experiencing only fleeting satisfaction, disappointment, and more reaching never ends until we experience a radical heart change—a value transformation.

It's easy to conclude we don't have quite enough. When we look around, there's always somebody we know—a friend, coworker, neighbor, or sibling—who has nicer things than we do. We're jealous, but we don't want to admit it, especially if we're Christians. Our dissatisfaction robs us of peace, kills our joy, and makes us competitors instead of lovers.

We need to stop and realize just how good we have it. More than three billion people on the planet, almost half the population, live on less than $3 a day, and 1.3 billion live in extreme poverty of less than $1.25 a day.[10] Eighty percent of the world's population lives on less than $10 a day.[11] More than 800 million don't have enough to eat,[12] and more than 750 million lack clean drinking water, a situation that spreads disease and death.[13]

These aren't just numbers. They're real people. Most of us are insulated from the crushing needs of others, so we're unaware of the plight of countless men, women, and children who struggle to make it through each day. Even if we were more aware, would we really care? Would we make changes to meet needs, even at our expense?

When we become sensitized to needs of others, things that never bothered us suddenly tear us apart. A few years ago, Jack Johnson released "The News," a song that describes a mother's attempts to protect her child from the harsh realities in the news. She tries to tell her little child that death and destruction are just fantasies, but she realizes something is missing in the telecast. She asks,

> "Why don't the newscasters cry when they read about the people who die?
>
> You'd think they could be decent enough to put just a tear in their eyes."[14]

When we watch the news or read online coverage, we're often exposed to events that have devastated people. Wars, natural disasters, murders, famine, fire, and other events have changed their lives forever, but most of us aren't moved by what we see and hear. Like the newsman, we've become numb to others' pain.

VALUE TRANSFORMATION

A value transformation changes our perceptions, which changes our motivations, which then changes our behavior. Our experience of God's grace—not just our knowledge of it, but having it explode in our hearts—turns selfish people into generous people. As we saw earlier, Paul put it this way: "Let nothing be done through selfish ambition or conceit, but in lowliness of mind let each esteem others better than himself. Let each of you look out not only for his own interests, but also for the interests of others" (Philippians 2:3–4).

> Our experience of God's grace—not just our knowledge of it, but having it explode in our hearts—turns selfish people into generous people.

A transformed person has God's view of people. We love the people God loves, and we care about the things God cares about. Bob Pierce is the founder of two outstanding aid organizations, World Vision International and Samaritan's Purse. Early in his travels, when he saw the suffering of children on the Korean island of Koje-do, he wrote these words in his Bible: "Let my heart be broken with the things that break the heart of God." What breaks your heart? What breaks mine?

The Bible has a lot to say about righteous and unrighteous people. We can differentiate them in many ways, but one of the most revealing is this: The righteous disadvantage themselves to benefit others, but the unrighteous disadvantage others to benefit themselves. The righteous—those who are learning to be Christ's disciples—are radically committed to being just and generous.

In our country, the word *justice* is most frequently associated with punishing the guilty, but in the Bible, the word includes two actions: punishing the guilty, yes, but also caring for the vulnerable. Who are the vulnerable? God spoke to the prophet Zechariah and identified four specific groups who need the care of God's people:

> Then the word of the Lord came to Zechariah, saying, "Thus says the Lord of hosts:
> 'Execute true justice,
> Show mercy and compassion
> Everyone to his brother.
> Do not oppress the widow or the fatherless,
> The alien or the poor.
> Let none of you plan evil in his heart
> Against his brother.'" (Zechariah 7:8–10)

The widow . . . the fatherless . . . the alien . . . the poor. Those groups weren't just concerns for biblical times. Author and pastor Tim Keller applies this passage to our culture:

In premodern, agrarian societies, these four groups [in Zechariah 7] had no social power. They lived at subsistence level and were only days from starvation if there was any famine, invasion, or even minor social unrest. Today this quartet would be expanded to include the refugee, the migrant worker, the homeless, and many single parents and elderly people.[15]

Being just and generous is costly, but it thrills God's heart when we display His essential nature of justice and generosity. And God promises to bless us richly if we'll turn from our selfishness to care for others. Through the prophet Isaiah, God told the people to stop being so petty and start devoting themselves to selfless service. He explained the incredible benefits:

"If you take away the yoke from your midst,
The pointing of the finger, and speaking wickedness,
If you extend your soul to the hungry
And satisfy the afflicted soul,
Then your light shall dawn in the darkness,
And your darkness shall be as the noonday.
The Lord will guide you continually,
And satisfy your soul in drought,
And strengthen your bones;
You shall be like a watered garden,
And like a spring of water, whose waters do not fail."
(Isaiah 58:9–11)

When Jesus tried to explain the concept of value transformation to religious leaders, He reminded them about loving God and loving their neighbor as they love themselves—with the same passion, commitment, joy, and sacrifice. One of them must have been squirming because he asked, "Who is my neighbor?" In response, Jesus told a story about a Samaritan (a race that was despised by the Jews) who was traveling on the road from Jerusalem to Jericho. A man had been beaten and robbed, and he was lying on the side of the road. Two religious leaders saw the man in a crumpled heap, but they didn't stop to help. When the Samaritan walked by, he had compassion for the man. He bandaged his wounds and put him on his donkey to take him to the nearest town. There, he paid for the man to have a room to convalesce for a few days, and he offered to pay even more if the man needed more time to heal. At the end of the story, Jesus asked, "So which of these three do you think was neighbor to him who fell among the thieves?"

The man who had quizzed Him replied, "He who showed mercy on him."

Jesus told him, "Go and do likewise" (Luke 10:29–37).

We see three distinct perspectives in Jesus' story. The thieves who robbed and beat the man believed, "What's yours is mine, and I'm going to take it." The two apathetic religious leaders who ignored the victim's many needs believed, "What's mine is mine, and I'm going to keep it." Those are the two most common perspectives among people today—even church people. We may be rich or poor, Democrats or Republicans, urban or rural, capitalists or socialists, management or labor, yet if our perspective hasn't been revolutionized from a worldly view to a kingdom view, we will always keep wanting more. We will continue to cling to what we have and want what others have. But there's a third life perspective in this story. The Samaritan's attitude was just and generous: "What's mine is yours, and I'm going to share it."

This level of generosity shouldn't be a surprise to anyone with even a casual understanding of the Bible, yet it's incredibly rare in the lives of Christians today. If we call Jesus "Lord," we're saying our possessions aren't our own, our time isn't our own, our resources aren't our own, our talents aren't our own, and our lives aren't our own. Paul wrote the

> If we call Jesus "Lord," we're saying our possessions aren't our own, our time isn't our own, our resources aren't our own, our talents aren't our own, and our lives aren't our own.

Corinthians, "Do you not know that your body is the temple of the Holy Spirit who is in you, whom you have from God, and you are not your own? For you were bought at a price; therefore glorify God in your body and in your spirit, which are God's" (1 Corinthians 6:19–20). And he told the Galatians that he so identified with the sacrifice of Christ that nothing mattered except his relationship with his Lord: "I have been crucified with Christ; it is no longer I who live, but Christ lives in me; and the life which I now live in the flesh I live by faith in the Son of God, who loved me and gave Himself for me" (Galatians 2:20).

Every time we approach the poor instead of rejecting them, every time we encourage someone rather than criticize, and every time we give sacrificially instead of holding back, we experience a little crucifixion, a tiny sacrifice of ourselves for someone else. We can always focus on ourselves, but whenever we choose to spend our time, money, and resources on someone in need, we are following the example of Jesus. We only truly live by dying, and we gain by giving.

What do we give? We give whatever God has put in our hands. Not long ago, I met with Leroy Graham, a physician who attends our church. We talked about all the confusion and debate about healthcare in America. There has been, and there will probably continue to be, a fierce debate about who should get healthcare what role the government should play. I told the doctor that I have a dream of providing outstanding healthcare for the poor in our community. We could mobilize the physicians, nurses, med techs, and people in all aspects of the profession. Dr. Graham is one of the leading pulmonologists in the city. He was near retirement, but I said, "You know you don't want to play golf every day after you retire. That might be fun for a week or two, but you'll get bored. What does God have for you in the next phase of your life?"

Dr. Graham caught the vision, and before long, God gave us a plan: Bridge Atlanta Health Center. Today, we've mobilized about 140 medical professionals. Many volunteer their services, and we have a fully functioning health care center for those in our community who don't have health insurance. What do you think America would look like if other churches did the same thing? The church would be "a lamp on a stand" and "a light on a hill." We could respond to some of the challenges in our society with a wonderful blend of compassion and effective, practical assistance . . . instead of waiting for the government to solve problems.

Throughout the Bible, one of the primary marks of a person who follows God is care for the weak, the poor, immigrants, widows, and orphans. (See Exodus 22:22–24; Isaiah 10:1–2; Jeremiah 22:3–5; Malachi 3:5; Luke 20:45–47; et al.) We can conclude that a heart in tune with God's is moved with compassion toward the vulnerable in our society, and a heart out of tune with God sees those people as irrelevant or as threats. This is one of the clearest distinctions between a believer and a disciple.

A GLOBAL PERSPECTIVE

When God transforms our values, we open our eyes to look beyond ourselves to see what God is doing—or wants to do—around the globe. That's what happened to Bob Pierce when he traveled to Korea, and it can happen to us anytime we're online or watching the news. God shows us ways we can touch people on the far side of the world.

Jace and Sarah Rabe came to our church several years ago. Jake was a successful commodities broker, but God gave him a bigger idea. He told me he had visited Benin in Africa. He said, "Pastor Dennis, God gave me a heart for that nation. The country's main export is cashews. I'm in the commodities business, and I've seen how other nations have taken advantage of the farmers in Benin. Brokers and politicians have gotten rich, but the farmers are still impoverished." Jace is a dreamer, but he's a dreamer who develops specific, workable plans. He told me, "I want to build a cashew processing factory in Benin that will invest profits back into the community there. That way, the workers will reap the benefits of their labor."

Jace's vision promised to make a big difference in that small nation, but he needed funding. He submitted a grant application to the Bill and Melinda Gates Foundation. They get thousands of requests, so they're careful about where they put their funds. A foundation administrator responded, "We're interested, but you'll need to prove your concept first. Build a factory and show operational progress, and then come back to us." Jace had to raise over a million dollars to build the first factory. He hired people to manage and run it, and he paid them a fair wage. His business plan included hiring some medical personnel to care for the factory workers and farm families. He planned to teach the farmers about microloans so they could grow their businesses. Eventually, they began digging water wells, and then they built a community center and local church.

Someday, we'll give an account to Jesus for all He has put in our hands.

What causes a young man with a wife and two little children to uproot their comfortable life in America to invest themselves in the people of a country most of us can't find on a map? It's simple: God gave them a value transformation that radically changed their perspective from local to global.

Someday, we'll give an account to Jesus for all He has put in our hands. It is a type of judgment—not the heaven or hell judgment for unbelievers, but Jesus' assessment of our faithfulness to use what He has entrusted to us. Paul describes that moment:

> According to the grace of God which was given to me, as a wise master builder I have laid the foundation, and another builds on it. But let each one take heed how he builds on it. For no other foundation can anyone lay than that which is laid, which is Jesus Christ. Now if anyone builds on this foundation with gold, silver, precious stones, wood, hay, straw, each one's work will become clear; for the Day will declare it, because it will be revealed by fire; and the fire will test each one's work, of what sort it is. If anyone's work which he has built on it endures, he will receive a reward. If anyone's work is burned, he will suffer loss; but he himself will be saved, yet so as through fire. (1 Corinthians 3:10–15)

On that day, believers will see a lot of their lives go up in smoke, but disciples will be left with the eternal treasure from a life that has made a difference. When our lives hit the fire, what will happen to all our money, possessions, and interests? What will last, and what will burn to a cinder? The only things that will last are the things that have eternal value—our investment in knowing, loving, and serving God by caring for the people He cares for.

If you faced this cleansing fire right now, what would burn and what would come out as pure gold and silver? When we imagine this future event, it changes the way we live today. We become more focused and full of purpose, with an eye on eternity in everything we do.

GENEROSITY: THE CIRCLE OF BLESSING

Another clear distinction between believers and disciples is generosity. Believers look for ways to hang on to what they have, and when they give, they give only what they can spare. Disciples give generously, sacrificially, and gladly.

The Bible provides a benchmark for our giving: the tithe, a tenth of what God entrusts to us. Another principle of giving is to offer the "first fruits," the first part of the harvest, as a sign of trust that God will bless the rest of the crop.

Many Christians see God's directive to tithe as only a law to obey rather than a willing opportunity to participate in God's activity. Certainly, Moses commanded the tithe in his laws concerning the children of Israel, but that's not how it started. Centuries before, Abraham fought against several kings who threatened his nephew Lot, and God gave him a glorious victory along with the spoils of war. When Abraham met Melchizedek, priest and king of Salem, Abraham gladly gave Melchizedek a tenth of all the spoils. There was no command involved; he gave it by faith with a glad and thankful heart. He was saying to God, "I realize all I have has come from you, and I acknowledge that all I am and all I have belong to you." He was grateful, so he gave.

Our use of money is a window on our hearts. People who are generous with their money and possessions reveal a heart gripped by the wonder of God's grace, but those who are stingy show their hearts haven't been transformed by the love of God. The tithe was a beginning point, a trigger to unleash the blessings of God in our lives. It was never just an arbitrary law. It was always a launching pad for us to experience more of God's abundance. When we refuse to tithe, we shut off the flow of blessings. It's as if we're telling God, "All I have is mine, not Yours." Through the prophet Malachi, God said this attitude robs Him of what He richly deserves.

> "Will a man rob God?
> Yet you have robbed Me!
> But you say,

ti EM_

just wanted to drop a note letting
you know that I love you.

I am sorry if I let you down.
The last week has been a whirl-
wind for me... I dropped the ball
with communicating. I am sorry
we did not talk about the change
regarding movers / the movers falling
through. This is my fault.
I should have done a better job
communicating. I was in my head.

It hurts my heart to know that I've
upset you +/or let you down.
I will do my best to be better.
I hope you can accept my apology.

You are a joy to be around, to
live with and a light in my
life. It makes me so sad knowing
their is any tension between us.

I am truly sorry. I love you.
And think me proud of you.
I pray that you know my heart.
I am truly sorry.

                XO XO keach.

'In what way have we robbed You?'
In tithes and offerings.
You are cursed with a curse,
For you have robbed Me,
Even this whole nation."
(Malachi 3:8–9)

God had given the law and the promise about tithing centuries before Malachi's time, but He repeats it again:

"Bring all the tithes into the storehouse,
That there may be food in My house,
And try Me now in this,"
Says the Lord of hosts,
"If I will not open for you the windows of heaven
And pour out for you such blessing
That there will not be room enough to receive it."
(Malachi 3:10)

So which comes first: the act of giving or the heart to give . . . the law or the love? It really doesn't matter how the process begins. Some people are so thrilled with all God has done for them that they eagerly give more than a tithe, even from the first day they trust in Christ. Others are a bit more skeptical, or perhaps cautious. They aren't sure God will really bless them if they give, but they're willing to take a risk. They find out God's Word is true. Oh, God may not open the floodgates of blessing the day they give, but they see Him open His hands of blessing sooner or later.

When we move into the New Testament, we find only a few references to tithing because the practice was so firmly established in the teaching of the Old Testament. Here, we see Jesus challenge His disciples to a higher level of thinking—and a deeper motivation—about giving. He moved them beyond tithing to sacrificial giving to further His kingdom on earth. The tithe was still part of their lives, but they learned the importance of giving above and beyond ten percent to sacrifice for others.

Paul explained the principle of giving by faith in his second letter to the Corinthians. He didn't focus on the law, the "have to" of giving. Instead, he encouraged that early church to think more deeply about God's amazing generosity as the stimulus for them to give. He wrote:

But this I say: He who sows sparingly will also reap sparingly, and he who sows bountifully will also reap bountifully. So let each one give as he purposes in his heart, not grudgingly or of necessity; for God loves a cheerful giver. And God is able to make all grace abound toward you, that you, always having all sufficiency in all things, may have an abundance for every good work. As it is written:

"He has dispersed abroad,
He has given to the poor;
His righteousness endures forever."

Now may He who supplies seed to the sower, and bread for food, supply and multiply the seed you have sown and increase the fruits of your righteousness, while you are enriched in everything for all liberality, which causes thanksgiving through us to God. (2 Corinthians 9:6–11)

We know our hearts are being transformed when our thought process changes from "How much can I keep and spend on myself?" to "How much can I give away?" We long for God to bless us, but not so we can have more stuff. We want God to bless us so we can be a blessing to others. We receive God's blessings as either reservoirs or rivers. Believers are reservoirs that hold essentially everything received (with maybe a small trickle of outflow). Disciples are rivers, always moving and continually in search of opportunities to overflow their banks with generosity!

What gives us joy? What brings deep, soul-satisfying contentment? Paul answered these questions in his first letter to Timothy: "Now godliness with contentment is great

> We know our hearts are being transformed when our thought process changes from "How much can I keep and spend on myself?" to "How much can I give away?"

gain. For we brought nothing into this world, and it is certain we can carry nothing out. And having food and clothing, with these we shall be content. But those who desire to be rich fall into temptation and a snare, and into many foolish and harmful lusts which drown men in destruction and perdition. For the love of money is a root of all kinds of evil, for which some have strayed from the faith in their greediness, and pierced themselves through with many sorrows" (1 Timothy 6:6–10).

Craig Hill is the founder of a ministry called Ancient Paths. He captures the concept of "godliness with contentment" in a concept he calls "the circle of God's blessing." He cites Psalm 25 as his inspiration: "Where is the man who fears the Lord? God will teach him how to choose the best. He shall live within God's circle of blessing, and his children shall inherit the earth" (Psalm 25:12–13, TLB).

Most people live with an "open circle," and their spending keeps expanding as their income and wealth increase. But Hill encourages us to live in a "closed circle" where we learn to be both content and generous. Here's how it works: Draw a circle, and inside it, write every tangible blessing you want God to give you: house, car, income, etc. You then make a commitment that as God pours out His blessings on you, the circle won't expand. You're making a vow to be content with the scope of your circle. You tithe whatever God gives within the circle, but you gladly give *everything* outside the circle.

The world tells us the measure of success is money, appearance, and IQ. But there's a big problem: If you value wealth, you'll always feel poor. If you value beauty, you'll be afraid of being ugly. If you value intelligence, you'll be terrified of looking dumb. It is reported that poet Rudyard Kipling told the graduating class of Montreal's McGill University, "If a person's scale of values is based primarily on material wealth, that person will be in difficulty all of his or her life. Do not pay much attention to fame, power, and money. Some day you will meet a person who cares for none of these, and then you will know how poor you are."

The Bible moves us beyond success to true significance. Success asks, "How can I add value to my own life?" but significance asks, "How can I add value to the lives of others?" Our commitment to live within the circle of blessing moves us from being preoccupied with our own success to focus instead on the significance we can have for God.

The commitment to live in the circle of blessing is a radical reversal of everything we see, read, and hear in the popular culture . . . and sadly, it's a radical reversal of some teaching in many churches. The culture tells us it's only right and good to upgrade when we prosper, but living with contentment in the circle of God's blessing stops the rat race of spending more on ourselves so we can have something bigger, finer, and faster. We don't think about the vulnerable and the poor. Instead our minds are filled with thoughts of the next purchase (and maybe worries of how we'll pay for it). That's not contentment! That's not joy! That's not a disciple's view of God's blessings!

Don't get me wrong. I'm not saying it's a sin to have nice things, but I *am* saying that being rich can insulate us from the needs of the poor and marginalized. That's a great danger. In the previously mentioned letter to Timothy, Paul told the young pastor how to guide those who are wealthy: "Command those who are rich in this present age not to be haughty, nor to trust in uncertain riches but in the living God, who gives us richly all things to enjoy. Let them do good, that they be rich in good works, ready to give, willing to share, storing up for themselves a good foundation for the time to come, that they may lay hold on eternal life" (1 Timothy 6:17–19). Like all of us, those who are wealthy need to imagine that day of judgment for their choices. On that day, their stinginess will be incinerated, but their generosity will glow like gold!

Do you consider yourself wealthy? If you live on more than $10 a day, you're in the top twenty percent of the world! Regardless of our financial status, Jesus pierces our hearts when He tells us, "For where your treasure is, there your heart will be also" (Matthew 6:21).

Do you want to know what's really in your heart? Peel back the layers of cultural assumptions and financial habits to uncover what you really value. What is the subject of your daydreams? That's what you really value. That's your treasure. What we do with our money and possessions reveals whether we *love God* more than our own pleasure and prestige, whether we *trust God* more than our wealth, and whether our *true purpose* is to expand the kingdom and touch the lives of the vulnerable or to advance our own agendas.

It's never too late to enter the circle of God's blessing. Another physician in our church had been living in an open circle, acquiring a bigger house, nicer cars, and more extravagant vacations as his income rose. When he learned about living in a closed circle of God's blessing, the concept suddenly made perfect sense. He realized his life had become absorbed in having things. He was making plenty of money, but it never seemed to be enough to satisfy him, and in fact, he had been living above his considerable means. He sold his palatial house and bought a modest home. He then had enough money to pay off all his debts. Before that revelation, he struggled with his motivation to give. Every dollar he gave conflicted with his goal of having more and bigger stuff. But after he began living in the circle of God's blessing, he started thinking much more about giving than getting, and his heart sings when his gifts make a difference in the lives of others.

In 2007, I read *The Blessed Life* by Robert Morris. He describes the spiritual principle of giving, and he shares stories of people who have given away material possessions far above the tithe. He wrote about particular times when God led him to give away everything he owned and trust Him to provide. When I finished the book, I felt inspired and challenged. I wondered, *Can I trust God enough to give everything away?* When I became a Christian, I sold my part of the business and gave everything away, but I hadn't done anything as radical since then. I was in my late 40s at the time, and I had accumulated a significant amount of money in my retirement account. Colleen and I would depend on that money someday, but I couldn't get the idea out of my mind of giving it all away and trusting God to provide. I told Colleen about my impression, and I was sure she would say, "Dennis, are you crazy? We can't do that!" But she didn't. She thought for a second and told me, "I'm in. If you think this is what God is leading us to do, let's do it."

I knew we would need to act quickly before the devil talked us out of it, so I called our financial advisor to give him the news. (Needless to say, our new commitment didn't go over well!) He reluctantly explained everything we would have to do with our 401Ks, taxes, and other funds. A few days later, after closing accounts and moving funds, we wrote the biggest check we'd ever given to the church!

Here we were: both of us 48 years old and starting our financial life over again. We had no idea how God might provide for us, but we were on an adventure of learning how to trust Him. Within two months, God orchestrated a series of events that brought in enough money to bring us up to the level where we'd been when we gave it all away, and since then, God has continued to pour out His blessings on our lives beyond anything we had ever dreamed possible!

I'm certainly not insisting that every person give everything away, but what I'm saying is that you need to be open to whatever God may lead you to do—even if it scares you! The key to walking with God is to keep your heart open—in this area of finances and every area of life—because He may want to do something radical through you like He did with the early disciples in the book of Acts! Remember, you're moving from being a believer to a disciple.

Some people don't want to give because they feel pressured by pastors. I understand that, so I assure the people who come to our church: "We don't need your money. Don't give because you think we're desperate and we're manipulating you. We're not and we don't."

Our church is committed to be a river that channels God's resources to care for the needy in our community and take the gospel to the world. A crazy goal I had when we started our church was to give $100 million while I was the pastor. At this point, we're almost halfway to that goal, about $50 million. We give twenty to twenty-five percent of the church's income to missions and caring for the vulnerable. In my wildest dreams, I never imagined a country boy like me would be able to participate in this kind of generosity. We've built orphanages and hospitals, we've rescued hundreds of girls and women from human trafficking, we've dug water wells in some of the most remote areas of the globe, we've provided food for the hungry and shelter for the homeless, and we've taken the message of Christ's love to people near and far.

Our church adopted Ogocha, Ethiopia, a town of about 100,000 people. The people there were dying of malnutrition and disease because they didn't have adequate water supplies. After a special Christmas offering, we were able to dig eighteen wells in the area. I told our people, "You can spend your money on another sweater for Uncle Joe or a necklace for Aunt Betty, or you can tell them you're giving the money to save the lives of men, women, and children in a town they never knew existed. Rerouting a little money will save hundreds and maybe thousands of people." When we went back the next year to see what clean water had done for them, we discovered the death rate had dropped by forty percent. We realized that giving our best gift to Christ at Christmas could save a lot of lives!

The next year, we traveled to the Ethiopian capital, Addis Ababa, where we saw a street lined with booths selling girls as sex slaves. We met the leaders of a ministry trying to rescue the girls, but they didn't have facilities for the girls after they fled their pimps. We used money donated by our people to build a church for the girls. The first Sunday, more than 400 girls came. Many of them got saved when they heard the gospel from people who cared for them instead of using and abusing them. We also built a dormitory where they could be safe, be deprogrammed, and find hope again.

Being part of these efforts is one of the great joys and privileges of my life. It's not our eloquence or administrative brilliance that has made all this happen; it's the shared vision and common purpose of a group of people who see themselves as God's powerful, flowing rivers instead of stagnant reservoirs.

Has the Lord captured your heart? Is He transforming your values so that you want to be just and generous? Does your heart break when you see the poor overlooked and the needy neglected? Do you see all you have as God's, and yourself as His steward to use it wisely? Believers and disciples have very different views of people, themselves, and their resources. Don't settle for being a believer. It seems safe, but it leaves you empty.

THINK ABOUT IT:

1. It's easy to watch the news and become numb to the stories and pictures of the desperate need of people around the world. What's the danger of being numb to the plight of such people?

2. Review Isaiah 58:9–11, and describe God's promise to those who share His heart for widows, orphans, the hungry, the sick, and immigrants.

3. How does "values transformation" take place in a person's life? What are some of the choices he or she inevitably faces? How have you faced them (or how do you plan to face them)?

4. What are some of the internal and external differences between tithing from a law motivation and tithing from a grace motivation?

5. Describe the "circle of God's blessing." How does this concept give you freedom and joy in being generous?

6. Would you ever consider giving everything away? Why or why not? How about considering giving a lot more than you're giving now?

7. On a scale of 0 (none) to 10 (absolutely), rate your commitment to be just and generous. Explain your answer. What needs to change to bring up your score?

CHAPTER 10

A DISCIPLE . . .
LIVES ON PURPOSE

I f we were really honest, I think most of us would admit that one of our chief goals is to avoid looking like a fool. We want people to see us as reasonably bright and competent. When Paul wrote his letter to the Ephesians, he recognized this core desire in the heart of every person. He told them, "So be careful how you live. Don't live like fools, but like those who are wise. Make the most of every opportunity in these evil days. Don't act thoughtlessly, but understand what the Lord wants you to do" (Ephesians 5:15–17, NLT).

We want to ask, "Paul, what are you talking about? What in the world would make us fools?" The answer he gives throughout the letter is that we are wise when we understand and follow God's divine purpose for our lives, and we're fools when we don't pursue it with all our hearts.

Paul hasn't been hard to grasp throughout this letter. Earlier, he wrote clearly, "It is in Christ that we find out who we are and what we are living for" (Ephesians 1:11, MSG). But he doesn't stop there. In the following chapter, he explained that the grace of God not only frees us from slavery to sin, but it propels us to invest our lives in God's great purposes: "God saved you by his grace when you believed. And you can't take credit for this; it is a gift from God. Salvation is not a reward for the good things we have done, so none of us can boast about it. For we are God's masterpiece.

He has created us anew in Christ Jesus, so we can do the good things he planned for us long ago" (Ephesians 2:8–10, NLT).

The plans of most people are narrow and self-focused, but God's plans for us are expansive, challenging, and thrilling. Before time began, God has had His eye on us, and He had plans for us to make a difference in individuals, families, and communities.

Too many of us fail to even ask, "Lord, why have You put me on earth? Why have You rescued me by Your grace? What do You want me to do with my life?" Or maybe we asked those questions years ago, but "the cares of this world, the deceitfulness of riches, and the desires for other things entering in choke the word, and it becomes unfruitful" (Mark 4:19). The great preacher Myles Munroe commented, "The greatest tragedy in life is not death, but life . . . life that fails to fulfill its purpose and potential."[16] It's dangerous to be alive and not know why you were given life.

In this final chapter, I want to bring a lot of the previously discussed concepts into focus to shine a light on our purpose, our reason to get up every morning, the compelling motive to make choices to honor God. By the way, I think it's perfectly fine to revisit some concepts. After all, God gave us four Gospels so we wouldn't miss His points!

ONE STEP BACK

When young people come to Christ, they have the whole world open to them. Unfortunately, many of them don't consider the questions about God's purposes. They just assume God will help them in whatever career they choose. And adults who trust in Jesus have already begun (and are often far down) the path of their careers. The idea of asking God to reveal His purpose isn't even on the radar. They spend their entire lives asking God to bless *their* choices without even considering if they are *God's* choices. They expect God to smooth the way to more and more success.

That's the thinking of a believer, not a disciple. People who are serious about following God pray, "Lord, not my will but Yours." No matter where God leads, they follow. God may tell them to stay where they are and be light and salt in their current profession, or He may redirect them to something they never dreamed of doing. The point is: it's up to Him, not us.

> God may tell them to stay where they are and be light and salt in their current profession, or He may redirect them to something they never dreamed of doing. The point is: it's up to Him, not us.

As I've observed people in every walk of life, I've identified five levels of purpose, from awful to awesome:

The first level: We do what we hate.

Whether it's conflict with family members, a career that saps our energies, or involvement in a school that seems like a dead end, our lives are filled with discouragement and resentment. Every day is a grind. We want to escape, but we can't shake the emptiness. On this level, we're miserable.

The second level: We do what we do.

Many people don't hate who they are or what they do, yet they aren't challenged or fulfilled. Day after day, we have the same routine, think the same thoughts, and see the same people. Life isn't horrible, but it isn't thrilling at all. At this level, we just go through the motions.

The third level: We do what we love.

Some people actually enjoy what they do each day. They have meaningful relationships, and they feel fulfilled in their studies or work. They experience some difficulties, but they're confident they can handle them. Life is good! For those who don't know God, this is usually the pinnacle of their sense of purpose. They assume this is the very best they can experience, but there are two more levels.

The fourth level: We do what God loves.

This is the transition from a believer to a disciple. Our hearts are increasingly in tune with God's heart, so we want to participate in His purposes. But this change comes at a cost because we must let go of what *we* love so we can become fully engaged in God's kingdom.

We might call this "the cross experience." It's where our will crosses God's will, and we're forced to make a decision about which path we choose. It's also where we look at Jesus on the cross as the ultimate example and source of strength as He lived out His choice: "Not My will but Yours be done."

The fifth level: We love to do what God loves.

From the outside, this level looks like the previous one, but our inner motivation changes. We become more than God's willing servants; we're His friends and partners. We want to please Him above all else. Our hearts are thrilled by what thrills Him, and our hearts break over the things that break His heart. This is "the sweet spot" for disciples where our hearts and our talents are put fully to use. Pastor and writer Frederick Buechner wrote, "The place God calls you is the place where your deep gladness and the world's hunger meet."[17] If we'll listen and respond, God will lead us to that place.

As we begin to live in the fifth level, we are more in touch with God's heart, and we tap into God's power—and He uses us in ways we never dreamed possible. This is what happened to the timid, fearful disciples when they gave themselves fully to the purposes of God. He used them to change the world!

THE PATH TO PURPOSE

When we respond to God's summons and invitation to become disciples and begin to take bold steps, He gives us encouraging signposts on the journey. First, we gain a new *focus* on what's really important. The scales come off our eyes and we see everything more clearly. We notice that we've spent a lot of time and energy on things that are either distractions or are flat wrong. God doesn't show us these things to crush us, but to invite us to a better relationship with Him, a better life, and a better future. We've been wasting far too much time on television shows, music, Facebook, Twitter, shopping, and other distractions, and we need to make better choices about how we invest our time. We've been spending our money on electronics that are obsolete in a year and other stuff we don't even need, and it's time to pour our money into the kingdom. We have been scattered, but now we become more focused.

A second signpost is a new sense of *peace*. This isn't the peace most people pursue when they think everything in life should fun and easy. When they don't get what they want, they get even more stressed and worried than before! Jesus promises a peace that's far deeper and wider than our circumstances. We have a wonderful peace with God because our sins are forgiven and His love never fails, and we have peace of mind because we're no longer struggling to compete to earn approval, attention, power, and control over others. Jesus told us, "Peace I leave with you, My peace I give to you; not as the world gives do I give to you. Let not your heart be troubled, neither let it be afraid" (John 14:27). You can expect His peace as you move along the path of purpose.

As we take steps to walk with God in the power of the Spirit, we begin to realize our *potential* that may been hidden before. Many of us have tried

> The glorious truth, though, is that we are new creations, with all the power and creativity of the Holy Spirit living in us!

incredibly hard to be a success, and perhaps have reached great heights. Others have felt blocked by a tragic family background, poor education, physical disabilities, or other hindrances—and all of us have suffered the effects of sin's enslavement. The glorious truth, though, is that we are new creations, with all the power and creativity of the Holy Spirit living in us! We may have felt helpless and hopeless in the past, but no longer. Our potential needs to be unleashed, or more accurately, it's a seed that needs to be planted. When I pick up an apple, the seeds are hidden from sight. If I take them out and plant them, each one produces an entire tree that will bear baskets of fruit each year for a long, long time. And each of those apples has the potential to multiply into more trees and more fruit. The potential of each tiny seed is practically limitless.

If you've trusted in Jesus, He has planted seeds of creativity, power, and love in you. Your calling—your privilege and responsibility—is to identify those seeds and plant them so they produce a magnificent harvest.

The Bible puts a lot of stock in another trait of disciples: *endurance.* Disciples face difficulties with optimism and tenacity. No matter how hard it gets, they don't quit.

What gives them the heart to keep going? A strong purpose enables us to endure. If I asked a hundred people to run ten miles, a few of them would be eager to go, but most would be very reluctant. They'd find dozens of excuses to keep from putting on their sneakers and getting on the road. But what if I told them, "If you finish the ten miles, I'll give you a million dollars"? I'm pretty sure a few more people would sign up!

What's the reward for our endurance? Paul was a tiger who endured incredible hardships, yet kept going, so he should know: "Therefore we do not lose heart. Even though our outward man is perishing, yet the inward man is being renewed day by day. For our light affliction, which is but for a moment, is working for us a far more exceeding and eternal weight of glory, while we do not look at the things which are seen, but at the things which are not seen. For the things which are seen are temporary, but the things which are not seen are eternal" (2 Corinthians 4:16–18). Paul had his eyes on a prize that wouldn't be realized until he saw Jesus face to face, and that was plenty of motivation for him to endure.

A shaky purpose can't keep us going when times are tough, but a powerful purpose gives us hope even in the darkest moments. God has told us what's coming. We have His precious and magnificent promises. If you know the end at the beginning, and you know what God is calling you to be and do, you're convinced that God has something bigger, higher, and greater than your present circumstances. When we forget this, we complain at every obstacle and we soon quit. But when we remember, we keep our eyes on the ultimate prize, and we endure to the end.

The last signpost of a disciple's path is *passion*. A strong sense of purpose inevitably fuels passion to accomplish it. To put it the other way: people without passion reveal that they don't have a compelling purpose. Actually, most people are passionate, but their emotions and energies are directed toward worldly pursuits of approval, possessions, and power. Disciples recognize the temptation to focus on these desires, and they continually reorient their hearts to follow Jesus. Passion for worldly goals starts well, but it ends in disaster. If we get what we're after, we become proud and self-absorbed. If we don't, we become deeply disappointed and sullen. Either way, we live with enormous stress. But God is a deep well of motivation, joy, and strength. As our hearts sing with joy over His power and love, we want everything we do to make a difference.

FIVE QUESTIONS

To discover and pursue God's purpose, we need to answer five crucial questions:

1. What's God's calling in your life?

When most people in churches hear the word "calling," they immediately think of the roles of a pastor, evangelist, or missionary, and they say, "Not me. I'm not called." But all Christians have been called by God to love Him and serve Him with all our hearts. God directs a few into full-time ministry, but He calls all of us to serve Him wherever He leads us. We can be right in the middle of God's will as an employer or employee, an entrepreneur or a mother, a hedge fund manager or a janitor. All vocations have eternal significance if we're following God's call and we do our work for His glory. We have been crafted by the hand of God so that we can make a difference in the destinies of others.

Professor and author Os Guinness insists that all believers belong to God all day, every day, whether we serve in the pastorate, at home, in offices, in the military, or in school. In his insightful book, *The Call,* Guinness says that God's design for us is all-encompassing: "God calls us to himself so decisively that everything we are, everything we do, and everything we have is invested with a special devotion and dynamism lived out as a response to his summons and service."[18]

When we find and follow God's calling, He doesn't promise to make everything smooth, easy, and efficient. Hardships and heartaches are always part of walking with God—just as Jesus, Peter, Paul, and every devoted disciple in history experienced! But God promises to weave everything that happens into a beautiful tapestry of meaning and joy. We may see only the back side of the weaving for a while, or maybe in this life, but we can be sure God is accomplishing something wonderful. One of the most quoted verses in the Bible confirms this promise. Paul wrote, "And we know that all things work together for good to those who love God, to those who are the called according to His purpose" (Romans 8:28). That's reassuring, isn't it? But we might understand it even more

But God promises to weave everything that happens into a beautiful tapestry of meaning and joy.

clearly if we read it with a negative twist: "And we know that all things become chaotic and destructive for those who don't put God first and who pursue their selfish ambitions." Those are two ways to live. Which one is more appealing to you? I thought so.

Far too often, we use God instead of loving and serving Him. We come up with our plans and we ask God to bless them. We don't ask Him for direction, and we don't consider His calling and His purpose for us. We just assume it's God's job to get on our train and make us successful. That's the way believers relate to God, and they're very disappointed when He doesn't jump through their hoops.

2. What's your burden?

One of the sure signs believers are turning into disciples is what keeps them awake at night. Believers may stay awake worried about what people think of them or say about them, how they can buy something they want, how to pay for what they've already bought, or countless other worries. Disciples have something else on their minds. They've come face to face with human needs, and their hearts are broken. Yes, they have concerns, but not about themselves . . . about vulnerable people who have no one to help them. They're not just concerned, though. They plan, they talk to others to get them involved, and they marshal resources to meet the need.

Pastor Andy Stanley observed, "Vision is born in the soul of a man or woman who is consumed with the tension between what is and what could be. Anyone who is emotionally involved—frustrated, brokenhearted, maybe even angry—about the way things are in light of the way they believe things could be, is a candidate for a vision. Visions form in the hearts of those who are dissatisfied with the status quo."[19]

A disciple's attitude is like Popeye who, when he reached the tipping point of exasperation, growled, "That's all I can stand. I can't stand no more!" I like to call this "holy discontent." What's your holy discontent? What's where your purpose begins.

A God-given burden inevitably results in action. When Colleen and I started seeking God about the vision for the church we would plant, we both sensed God asking us to identify our "holy discontent"—the pressing need that we couldn't walk away from. One day while reading through the book of Acts, I sensed God calling attention to the very last words of Jesus recorded in the Bible: "But you shall receive power when the Holy Spirit comes upon you; and you shall be my witnesses in Jerusalem, and in all Judaea and Samaria, and to the ends of the earth" (Acts 1:8).

Suddenly I realized God was saying there are four areas every disciple should be impacting throughout their lives. For many years, I had been feeling a strong burden for these areas, but I hadn't realized my purpose (and our church's purpose) was found right there in those words! I quickly wrote down what eventually would become the four pillars of the vision of our church:

- Building strong families,
- Transforming communities,
- Reconciling cultures, and
- World missions.

For us, Jerusalem represented our families, Judea represented the community around us, Samaria represented other cultures that were different from our own, and the ends of the earth was simply world missions. I remember thinking that if our church could just give ourselves to these four areas, we would be carrying out the Great Commission in its entirety.

Every day, these four purposes are the burdens that drive us to make a difference in our world. If you were to visit Victory, you would find countless disciples working to strengthen families in every way. You would see other disciples reaching out to every area of the community, from prisons to schools to nursing homes, to address countless areas of need where people have been forgotten. Perhaps the most surprising feature of the church is that over 140 nations worship together every week displaying the power of love through transformed hearts. Besides giving twenty to twenty-five percent of our annual budget to world missions and the needy, we also see hundreds of disciples going to the mission field every month to serve in some capacity. It's amazing how much happens when you match your heart with God's purposes!

No matter where we live or work, God puts the needs of others on our hearts. Then He won't let us rest until something is moving forward to meet those needs. That's a disciple's burden.

3. What's the cost we have to pay?

Believers may have been with us up to this point in the chapter, but at this step they may disappear! Many are in as long as they see the benefits, but the cost? No thanks. Fulfilling our calling, however, always comes at a price. We have to sacrifice something to achieve something else. We have to let go of the good to grab hold of the glorious. Today, churches are filled with people whose only thought is what God can do for them. They want all the privileges and blessings, but they don't understand the cost of discipleship—or if they understand it, they don't want it!

During a period of Jesus' ministry, He was incredibly popular. People were amazed when He turned a boy's sack lunch into a feast for 5000 men (probably closer to 20,000 in total, including the women and children). The people were so impressed that they wanted to make Him their king right then! But Jesus knew they didn't really understand Him or the purpose of His miracles. Instead of basking in their adulation, Jesus retreated into the mountains to pray. That night as the disciples rowed across the lake, a storm scared them. In the middle of the night, they saw Jesus walking on the water toward them. The Lord of the universe wasn't unsettled by a storm. He got in the boat, and they arrived on the other side.

The next day, the multitudes of people were eager to find Jesus, but they were confused. How had Jesus gotten to the other side of the lake? They made the trek around the shore to find Him, and they expected Him to feed them again. They demanded physical bread, but Jesus offered them spiritual food they needed far more; He offered himself, "the bread of life." An argument ensued when the people realized they weren't going to get what they wanted, and they became hostile. Jesus told them bluntly, "Most assuredly, I say to you, unless you eat the flesh of the Son of Man and drink His blood, you have no life in you. Whoever eats My flesh and drinks My blood has eternal life, and I will raise him up at the last day. For My flesh is food indeed, and My blood is drink indeed. He who eats My flesh and drinks My blood abides in Me, and I in him" (John 6:53–56). The enormous crowd was so bothered by this statement they quickly disbursed and went home. Eventually only the Twelve were left, and on the suddenly lonely hillside, Jesus asked them, "Do you also want to go away?"

At some points in our walks with Jesus, we'll feel like bailing out because the cost seems too high. In those moments, Jesus turns to us and asks, "Do you also want to go away?" We then have to dig deep to figure out why we're following Jesus in the first place. Did we count the cost?

Jesus suffered misunderstanding, slander, betrayal, torture, and a cruel death. He says to all of us, "Follow Me." If we truly follow Him, do we expect to participate in at least a semblance of His suffering? We should. The cost is always higher than we imagined, but the blessings of faithfulness are always higher still.

Some might ask, "Dennis, what cost are you talking about?" Great question. Let me give you several categories. First, relationships. Who is your Lord? Who is the one you want to please more than anyone else? Some of us are far more devoted to our spouse, our parents, our kids, or our boyfriend or girlfriend than to Jesus. We may want their love because we feel insecure, or we may want their love because our highest dream, our biggest purpose, is to have a happy marriage and great kids. Single people often dream of finding the perfect person, but married people often become so disillusioned with their spouse they pour all their hopes and dreams into their children. As we saw in an earlier chapter, Jesus spoke bluntly and clearly when He said we have to "hate" our fathers, mothers, brothers, sisters, husbands, wives, and kids if we want to be His disciples. And as we said, "hate" doesn't mean we're cruel to them; it means our love for Jesus surpasses all other relationships. Sooner or later (and probably sooner), those who want to be Christ's disciples have to pay the price in relationships and put Jesus at the top of their affections. It's always a tough test.

Being a disciple also involves paying a price in material possessions. We no longer give Jesus what we can easily afford and spend all the rest (and more) on ourselves. We realize that *all* we have belongs to God, and He has entrusted it to us as His stewards. Believers live by Edward Norton's often-quoted mantra of self-absorption: "We buy things we don't need with money we don't have to impress people we don't like." Disciples have a very different calculus about money and possessions. They dream about making an impact for the kingdom, so they make financial decisions to accomplish that goal.

Disciples spend less than they make so they can invest more in God's work.

Disciples spend less than they make so they can invest more in God's work. Over time, as they get promotions and raises, they limit their spending so they can give even more away. Some pastors teach that following God's call about spending and giving guarantees wealth. That would be news to Jesus, the disciples, the refugees in the first century who took the gospel to the world, and countless others who gladly lived with less because they delighted in God more. The guarantee isn't a promise of financial riches, but spiritual riches. We can count on that.

Similarly, we pay a price in our level of comfort. In our culture, we expect (or demand) a life of convenience. Everything in our world is designed to make life easy. Some people have told me they changed churches because the seats in their previous one weren't comfortable enough, and plenty of people have left a church because the pastor didn't let them out in time to beat the crowds to the restaurant. When we become disciples, we enter into other people's messy lives. Their addictions, disease, and resentments take a lot of our time and energy—first to figure out what in the world is going on and then to help them take steps toward hope and healing. Disciples make sacrifices, including their expectations of a comfortable life.

If we stay in a "holy huddle" of people who think and act just like us, we won't take the risk of losing our popularity, which is another price disciples have to pay. But if we engage people in our culture, we'll move toward addicts, gay people, foreigners, the poor, and people from other nations. When some of them find out we're Christians, they may despise us because they've been hurt before by believers. And when we move toward those people and actually become friends with them, some of the people in the church will accuse us of "lowering our standards" or other such rubbish. Jesus caught flak from all sides, but He never stopped moving toward people.

4. How do we prepare to live according to God's purpose?

We don't just wake up one day and become fully engaged in fulfilling God's purpose for us. Like any construction, art, or gardening project, progress takes time, attention, and resources. If you were a painter and you wanted to produce a masterpiece, you'd sharpen your skills, find the right subject and setting, buy all the materials you'd need, and carve out the time. In the same way, disciples realize they need to sharpen their skills, find the right mentors, and make changes in their habits. It is an intentional and ongoing process to invest the time, education, and other resources they'll need so they can follow their burden and become God's partner in changing lives.

If we pay attention, we may discover that God has already put a lot of the pieces together in preparation for our calling. When my good friend Nicole Boone graduated with honors from the master's program in education at the University of Virginia, she was planning to become an outstanding educator. But God redirected her plans. He began to speak to her about the plight of children in South Africa, kids who had been orphaned by HIV-AIDS. Suddenly, Nicole realized her education and experiences were God's preparation to help those children. She had to think and pray to clarify her calling, her burden, and the cost she'd have to pay. At 25, she understood that responding to God's calling would cost her dearly in terms of relationships and finances, as well as in comfort and professional prestige. She was also considering moving to a land decimated by disease where she might not find many available (or desirable) bachelors.

Nicole faced those decisions more than fifteen years ago, and she hasn't looked back. God had prepared her for great things, and she was willing to answer His call to redirect the trajectory of her life to care for needy children in a foreign land. She is part of Goshen International, a wonderful ministry that cares for and educates orphans. Nicole knows God can intervene again at any time. Her training and experience are preparation, either for more effectiveness in doing what she's doing now, or perhaps for something different. She's listening to God and responding to His call.

5. What's the risk of pursuing God's purpose?

Some people are adrenaline junkies who live for the next breathtaking adventure! But most of us are much more cautious. We want to minimize risk . . . and some of us avoid it at all costs. The Christian life is certainly an adventure. Every faithful person in the Bible took great risks to obey God's voice and follow His commands. Next to the Bible, the book that has sold more copies than any other in history is John Bunyan's *Pilgrim's Progress*, an allegory of the joys and struggles of following Jesus.

Hebrews 11 is often called "God's Hall of Faith" because it chronicles the heroism of numerous men and women of God. In times of darkness and opposition, those individuals trusted God and accepted risks, understanding there were no guarantees of miraculous intervention. They saw incredible miracles . . . although not all of them experienced a happy ending. The writer of Hebrews begins with positive comments, but then suddenly changes gears:

And what more shall I say? For the time would fail me to tell of Gideon and Barak and Samson and Jephthah, also of David and Samuel and the prophets: who through faith subdued kingdoms, worked righteousness, obtained promises, stopped the mouths of lions, quenched the violence of fire, escaped the edge of the sword, out of weakness were made strong, became valiant in battle, turned to flight the armies of the aliens. Women received their dead raised to life again. Others were tortured, not accepting deliverance, that they might obtain a better resurrection. Still others had trial of mockings and scourgings, yes, and of chains and imprisonment. They were stoned, they were sawn in two, were tempted, were slain with the sword. They wandered about in sheepskins and goatskins, being destitute, afflicted, tormented— of whom the world was not worthy. They wandered in deserts and mountains, in dens and caves of the earth. (Hebrews 11:32–38)

Sawn in two? Yes, and abandoned in sickness and poverty. They knew the risks, and they accepted the outcome. The writer holds up these courageous disciples as examples for us. They lived for something much bigger than success, pleasure, and approval. "And all these, having obtained a good testimony through faith, did not receive the promise, God having provided something better for us, that they should not be made perfect apart from us" (Hebrews 11:39–40).

When God touched me and I decided to become a disciple, I had big choices to make, and those choices involved great risk. I left a comfortable life and a profitable career to move to a city where I knew a grand total of one person. There, I took the risk of getting involved in the lives of broken people . . . who sometimes threatened my life. When I heard God's call to be a pastor, I took the risk of moving to Tulsa to invest years in preparation . . . not knowing if anyone would ever want someone like me to be their pastor. Like Peter, I often felt God was asking me to step out of the boat and onto the sea. Again and again, I swallowed hard and said, "Okay, Lord. I'm stepping out of the boat." Many times, like Peter, I doubted and began to sink, but Jesus has stretched out His hand to catch me every time. Oh, I've gotten wet plenty of times, but He has never let me drown in doubt and discouragement.

Have you stepped out of the boat, or are you too afraid to trust Jesus? Be honest. Are you holding back because you don't want to take too much risk, be too zealous for Jesus, and have your friends think you're too weird? Those doubts and fears are normal . . . and believers stay stuck in them. Disciples look at the wind and waves, but they also hear Jesus saying, "Step out of the boat. You can trust Me. I'm here for you." They trust Him and take a step.

NOW WHAT?

What has God been saying to you as you've studied the ten traits of a disciple? Has your heart been warmed by His love and challenged by His commands? Are still satisfied with being only a believer, or has the Holy Spirit enflamed your desire to follow Jesus no matter what He asks of you? Jesus' last command was to "make disciples." The world hasn't been reached or changed by believers, but it's been revolutionized by Jesus' disciples. The Twelve have multiplied by the word of truth and sacrificial service to include almost two billion across the world today.

> The world hasn't been reached or changed by believers, but it's been revolutionized by Jesus' disciples.

Too many churches are more interested in drawing a crowd than pointing people to the demands and commands of being Christ's disciples. If your church is promoting this book, your pastor and your church are part of the solution, not the problem.

We're in a war for the souls of individuals and the values of our culture. The traits we've examined in this book are designed to motivate people to get off the sidelines and into the fight, to stop being self-focused and begin to care about others, to value Jesus more than comfort and things, to become a flowing channel of God's love and power . . . to be transformed from a basic believer into a devoted disciple.

Are you in? I thought so.

THINK ABOUT IT:

1. Review the five levels of engaging in life. Which of them represented your life ten years ago . . . two years ago . . . and represent it today? Which one do you want to represent your future? Explain your answer.

2. Take a minute to dream: What might be your God-given potential as a disciple of Christ? What would someone who loves you and believes in you say about your potential?

3. What are some ways you can identify the focus of a person's passion? What does it mean to have a passion for Jesus and His kingdom?

4. What has God called you to be and do? How do you know? How are you pursuing this calling?

5. What are some of the costs you currently face to fulfill your calling? (What are some additional costs you may face if you become more intent on fulfilling it?)

6. How can you prepare yourself—motivation, skills, training, etc.—to be a more effective disciple?

7. On a scale of 0 (none) to 10 (to the max), how much are you passionately committed to fulfill God's calling in your life? Explain your answer. What needs to change?

ENDNOTES

1   "What Do Americans Believe about Jesus? 5 Popular
     Beliefs," Barna Group, *Articles in Faith and Christianity*,
     April 1, 2015, https://www.barna.com/research/
     what-do-americans-believe-about-jesus-5-popular-beliefs/#

2   Dietrich Bonhoeffer, *The Cost of Discipleship* (New York:
     Touchstone, 1959), p. 87.

3   Agata Blaszczak-Boxe, "Americans more depressed now than de-
     cades ago," CBS News, October 2, 2014, http://www.cbsnews.com/
     news/americans-more-depressed-now-than-decades-ago/

4   Lee Strobel, *The Case for Christ* (Grand Rapids: Zondervan, 1998),
     p. 97.

5   Marina Koren, "Where the World's Slaves Live," *The Atlantic*, May
     31, 2016, https://www.theatlantic.com/news/archive/2016/05/
     where-the-worlds-slaves-live/484994/

6   Cited at jan.ucc.nau.edu/~jsa3/hum355/readings/ellul.htm.

7   Monita Rajpal, "The Power of Advertising," CNN, cited on www.
     cnn.com/2010/WORLD/europe/09/22/power.of.advertising/in-
     dex.html

8   *Festival Letters*, quoted by Eusebius, *Ecclesiastical History* 7.22, 1965
     ed.

9   Rodney Stark, *The Rise of Christianity* (HarperOne: New York,
     1996), pp. 7, 73-94.

10 United Nations Development Programme. "Sustaining Human Progress: Reducing Vulnerabilities and Building Resilience." Human Development Report, 2014. Web Accessed February 25, 2015.

11 United Nations. "The Millennium Development Goals Report 2007." United Nations, 2007. Web Accessed April 29, 2014.

12 FAO, IFAD, and WFP. "The State of Food Insecurity in the World 2014. Strengthening the enabling environment for food security and nutrition." Food and Agriculture Organization of the UN, 2014. Web Accessed February 25, 2015.

13 World Health Organization and UNICEF Joint Monitoring Programme (JMP). "Progress on Drinking Water and Sanitation, 2014 Update." 2014. Web Accessed February 25, 2015.

14 Jack Johnson, "The News," *Brushfire Fairytales*, Enjoy Records, 2001.

15 Timothy Keller, *Generous Justice* (New York: Dutton, 2010), p. 4.

16 Myles Munroe, *Releasing Your Potential: Exposing the Hidden You* (Shippensburg, PA: Destiny Image, 1992), p. 32.

17 Frederick Buechner, *Wishful Thinking* (New York: HarperCollins, 1973), p. 95.

18 Os Guinness, *The Call*, (Nashville: Word, 1998), p. 4.

19 Andy Stanley, *Visioneering* (New York: Multnomah, 1999), p. 17.

HOW TO LEAD A GROUP USING *10*

This book is designed for individual study, small groups, and classes. The best way to absorb and apply these principles is for each person to individually study and answer the questions at the end of each chapter then to discuss them in either a class or a group environment.

Each chapter's questions are designed to promote reflection, discussion, and application. Order enough copies of the book for each person to have a copy. For couples, encourage both to have their own book so they can record their individual reflections.

A recommended schedule for a small group or class might be:

Week 1

Introduce the material. As a group leader, tell your story of finding and fulfilling God's dream, share your hopes for the group, and provide books for each person. Encourage people to read the assigned chapter each week and answer the questions.

Weeks 2–11

Each week, introduce the topic for the week and share a story of how God has used the principles in your life. In small groups, lead people through a discussion of the questions at the end of the chapter. In classes, teach the principles in each chapter, use personal illustrations, and invite discussion.

PERSONALIZE EACH LESSON

Ask people in the group to share their responses to the questions that meant the most to them that week. Make sure you personalize the principles and applications. At least once in each group meeting, add your own story to illustrate a particular point.

Make the Scriptures come alive. Far too often, we read the Bible like it's a phone book, with little or no emotion. Paint a vivid picture for people. Provide insights about the context of people's encounters with God, and help those in your class or group sense the emotions of specific people in each scene.

FOCUS ON APPLICATION

The questions at the end of each chapter and your encouragement to group members to be authentic will help your group take big steps to apply the principles they're learning. Share how you are applying the principles in particular chapters each week, and encourage them to take steps of growth, too.

THREE TYPES OF QUESTIONS

If you have led groups for a few years, you already understand the importance of using open questions to stimulate discussion. Three types of questions are *limiting, leading,* and *open.* Many of the questions at the end of each lesson are open questions.

Limiting questions focus on an obvious answer, such as, "What does Jesus call himself in John 10:11?" They don't stimulate reflection or discussion. If you want to use questions like these, follow them with thought-provoking, open questions.

Leading questions require the listener to guess what the leader has in mind, such as, "Why did Jesus use the metaphor of a shepherd in John

10?" (He was probably alluding to a passage in Ezekiel, but many people don't know that.) The teacher who asks a leading question has a definite answer in mind. Instead of asking this kind of question, you should just teach the point and perhaps ask an open question about the point you have made.

Open questions usually don't have right or wrong answers. They stimulate thinking, and they are far less threatening because the person answering doesn't risk ridicule for being wrong. These questions often begin with "Why do you think...?" or "What are some reasons that...?" or "How would you have felt in that situation?"

PREPARATION

As you prepare to teach this material in a group or class, consider these steps:

1. Carefully and thoughtfully read the book. Make notes, highlight key sections, quotes, or stories, and complete the reflection section at the end of each chapter. This will familiarize you with the entire scope of the content.

2. As you prepare for each week's class or group, read the corresponding chapter again and make additional notes.

3. Tailor the amount of content to the time allotted. If you don't have time to cover all the questions, pick the ones that are most important to your group.

4. Add your own stories to personalize the message and add impact.

5. Before and during your preparation, ask God to give you wisdom, clarity, and power. Trust him to use your group to change people's lives.

6. Most people will get far more out of the group if they read the chapter and complete the reflection each week. Order books before the group or class begins or after the first week.

ABOUT THE AUTHOR

Dennis Rouse grew up in a small suburb of Atlanta, Georgia, during the Civil Rights era when the South was going through a major shift of integrating schools and communities. In 1970, as an eighth-grade student, he found himself as the only white person in his homeroom class. For the first time, he discovered what it felt like to live as a minority in America.

In his early 20's, after leaving the business world and answering a call to the ministry, Dennis reflected on his experience and remembered the famous statement by Martin Luther King, Jr.: "11:00 on Sunday morning is the most segregated hour in America." He began to wonder if it was possible for the church to change the way we worship and how we represent ourselves to the community.

In 1990, God drew Dennis and his wife Colleen back to Atlanta to start a church with a vision based on the last words spoken by Jesus in Acts 1:8, and Victory World Church was born. God spoke to Dennis and Colleen about four major areas of influence—these are essential if the church is to fulfill the Great Commission. The four pillars of Victory are: *building strong families, transforming the community, reconciling cultures,* and *impacting nations.*

In the years since it began, Victory has become one of the largest multicultural churches in America with more than 16,000 members representing over 140 nationalities. Dennis and the church have a strong emphasis of moving people from just being believers in Jesus to becoming His disciples.

Pastor Dennis's life is based on three central principles: *simplicity, sincerity,* and *sacrifice.* He and Colleen have a clear and compelling goal to help the global church and its leaders become more relevant and equipped to reach emerging generations. Dennis is a sought-after speaker both nationally and internationally on many different topics, including the future of the church, how to build a multicultural church, and leading the next generation.

RESOURCES

To dive deeper and continue learning how to move from a believer to a disciple, stay connected with Pastor Dennis Rouse as he speaks on discipleship and other topics.

Facebook, Instagram and Twitter
@dennisvrouse

Victory World Church
Senior Pastor Dennis Rouse
@victoryatl

10 Resources

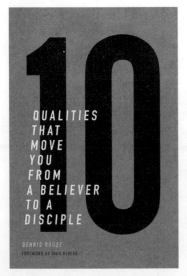

The goal of this book is to see as many believers as possible become disciples, and Pastor Dennis Rouse would like to get it into the hands of people worldwide. The book is designed for individual study, small groups or classes.

Bulk purchasing discounts are available for churches, groups, and organizations.

In addition to the book, a corresponding DVD curriculum will be available.

To order more copies of this book, the DVD curriculum or for more info, go to **10qualities.com**